Listed Buildings in Sheffield

Barbara A. West

Paradise Square — east side

Listed Buildings
in Sheffield

Barbara A. West

The **Hallamshire** Press 1998

Published by The Hallamshire Press
The Hallamshire Press is an imprint of
Interleaf Productions Limited
Broom Hall
Sheffield S10 2DR
England

Typeset by Interleaf Productions Limited and printed by
The Cromwell Press, Trowbridge, Wiltshire.

British Library Cataloguing in Publication Data:

West, Barbara A.
    Listed buildings
    1. Historic buildings
    I. Title
    720.9

ISBN   1-874718-32-6

Contents

Acknowledgements

I am very grateful for the help given to me by the owners of these buildings and to those who permitted me to photograph them, in particular to:

Beauchief Hall (E.D.P. Limited)
Broom Hall (David Mellor)
Carbrook Hall
Endcliffe Hall, T.A.V.R.
King Edward VII School
Lyceum Theatre
Mappin Art Gallery
Sanderson Kayser
Sharrow Snuff Mills
Sheffield Museums
St Mary's Beighton (Mrs Flinders)
St Mary's Bramall Lane (Dennis Fielding)

Also to Eva Wilkinson, Graham Hague, Mrs A. Smith, Tony and Rene Smith and Sheffield City Libraries for their help with the research.

Introduction

This latest list, of December 12th 1995, replaces the previous list of 1973, 382 buildings and structures have been added and a few removed or downgraded, for example, a pump and trough near Grange farmhouse, Hereward's Road, Norton, Grade II listed, have been stolen, some places have been demolished and others delisted for various reasons.

The new list has changed, in that descriptions have been updated and improved, using information provided by the research and surveys done by The Royal Commission on the Historic Monuments of England, and English Heritage.

Buildings are listed because they are considered to be of special architectural or historical interest, by the Department of National Heritage. They represent the growth and expansion of the town, which has evolved since mediaeval times to the present era, especially in connection with the iron and steel industry that made Sheffield the city it is today.

Most listed buildings are still in use but often in a different way from the original, for example, Carbrook Hall is now a Public House, Broom Hall is office accommodation and Norton Hall became a hospital.

Very little pre-1700 survives in Sheffield today. In the City Centre there are parts of the Cathedral that date back to the 15th century and, under Castle Market, there are some foundations of the Castle that remain as evidence of the mediaeval settlements around the River Don in the Lady's Bridge area. However, the street names remain to give us some guidance as to the layout, such as Castle Green, Waingate, Fargate and the Wicker.

The history of Sheffield has evolved around the iron and steel making industry, indeed, from as early as the 13th century, there is evidence of the existence of small workshops in South Yorkshire. Water-powered tools were built beside the rivers that flow into the Don and Sheaf, the Rivelin, Porter and Loxley rivers have their origins in the Pennines, where the rainfall is plentiful. Their valley bottoms contain remains of dams and water mills for grinding flour, driving bellows for furnaces, operating hammers and for turning grinding wheels. Cottage industries developed in these isolated surroundings which provided wood, charcoal and coal for the furnaces, clay for the crucibles and millstone grit for the grinding wheels. Very little remains of these early cutlers' workshops but the Shepherd Wheel, in the Porter Valley, and the Abbeydale Industrial Hamlet, on the River Sheaf, were made into museums to show

how the manufacturers worked and lived. Unfortunately, these sites have been closed since April 1997 pending new arrangements for their administration. As yet there is no date for re-opening but it is likely during 1998.

The earliest surviving houses were timber framed, as can be seen from the Old Queens Head and Bishops' House. The 17th and 18th centuries brought much sturdier, stone built houses, such as Beauchief Hall and The Oakes in Norton. These were quality houses, built by wealthy gentlemen, and have survived for that reason.

On the outskirts of Sheffield, early stone churches, such as St Mary's at Beighton, St James at Norton, Beauchief Abbey and Ecclesfield church have survived, also, in the surrounding countryside, are many farmhouses and cottages from the 18th century. They were built of local sandstone with stone mullion windows and heavy, sandstone roof tiles. They remain due to their continued use as dwellings surrounded by farmland, unlike the town houses which were demolished for road widening or to make place for grander buildings. Sheffield town centre spread up to, and developed around, the then parish church of St Peter with dwellings in Queens Street and Paradise Square.

Away from the town centre, grand houses were built by landed gentry, like the Sitwells of Renishaw who came to Mount Pleasant, and by the new steel magnates of the 19th century, such as John Brown who redeveloped Endcliffe Hall and Mark Firth who built Oakbrook. Many large houses in Ranmoor were built for the wealthy industrialists of that time.

The new list particularly reflects the importance of the 19th century in the history of Sheffield. Not only was some of the housing elegant but many of the factories too were designed on classical, architectural lines, such as Globe Works (1825) and Sheaf Works, now a public house, near the canal basin. The Gateway to Green Lane Works and the Midland Bank in Church Street, the Gas Offices in Commercial Street and even schools, like King Edward VII in Broomhill were in a neo-classical style.

Life after death was also cared for with the General Cemetery, designed originally by Samuel Worth and opened in 1836. It consisted of an Egyptian Gateway on Cemetery Road, the registrars house (notice the windows with converging verticals) the non-conformist chapel, designed in a classical style, the catacombs and the buildings and grand entrance at the end of Cemetery Avenue.

Sheffield grew rapidly in the 18th and 19th centuries with the building of steel factories in the Don Valley and terraced housing for the workers, and in this, the 20th century, there has been a greater variety of building styles than ever before. There have been some controversial listings, such as the University Arts Tower, and the listing of Park Hill flats is at present under discussion. However, it is good to know that the buildings in the following pages are being nurtured and preserved as reminders of Sheffield's heritage.

Barbara A. West
1998

Buildings of Special Architectural or Historical Interest

A listed building is one that has been judged to be of special architectural or historical interest by the Department of the Environment. The inspection of such buildings is carried out by the Historic Buildings and Monuments Commission in England, and the Scottish and Welsh Offices in Scotland and Wales respectively. It is a classification which carries both privileges and responsibilities. A listed building is protected by law against demolition without consent, and against alteration without permission.

All buildings constructed before 1700 and which are still in their original design are eligible for listing. Many buildings dated between 1700 and 1840 are selected for listing and, from 1840 onwards, only buildings of quality and character are listed.

There are three categories. An edifice of outstanding national importance is given Grade I. Those of outstanding regional importance are Grade II* (grade two star). All others are listed as Grade II. The first Listing Survey started in 1947, took twenty years to complete and it classified 150,000 buildings. The latest survey was completed by the Department of National Heritage on December 12th, 1995.

Churches were listed as A, B and C but they are now labelled the same as secular buildings, Grade I, II*, and II. The normal rules for listed buildings do not apply to churches in ecclesiastical use.

Sheffield has over 1,000 Listed Buildings. Of these, only the Town Hall, the Cathedral of Saints Peter and Paul, and Abbeydale Industrial Hamlet are in the Grade I category. There are 48 Grade II* buildings which include timber-framed houses such as Bishop's House in Norton Lees Lane, Broom Hall, and the Old Queen's Head public house in Pond Hill. There are over 852 Grade II listed buildings in Sheffield, these are catalogued at the back of this book. The list is held in the Department of Land and Planning in the Town Hall, and in the local studies department of the Central Library.

If you intend to explore some of these please remember that many are private houses so please respect the privacy of the residents.

Listed Building Consent

A Listed Building does not have to remain exactly the same for ever, but written approval must be obtained before any alterations are made which would affect the character and appearance of the property and its immediate environment, or, before demolishing the whole or part of the building.

It is an offence, punishable by a fine or up to a year's imprisonment or both, to demolish or alter a Listed Building without consent.

Changes to the design of the windows, external doors and rendering or painting of the external walls normally requires consent. Removing internal fixtures, such as oak panelling or an original fireplace may not be permitted. Most owners of Listed Buildings are proud to be associated with them but, occasionally, when planning permission is sought to extend, or make alterations to the original to suit their particular needs, they can find themselves at variance with the Conservation Officer. The Listed Property Owners Club was set up three years ago to support owners with disputes over planning permission. There are now over 2,000 members, they can be contacted on 01795 844 939.

Owners are expected to keep Listed Buildings in good condition using exactly matching materials for repairs. If the City Council thinks that work is urgently required for the preservation of an unoccupied Listed Building, it can carry out this work and recover the cost from the owner. These powers are only used when the owner fails to undertake repairs after requests from the City Council. Grants are sometimes available on application to the Directors of Planning and Design.

Grade I Listed Buildings

The Town Hall

Pinstone Street and Surrey Street

The present Town Hall was built in the Victorian era to replace the former Town Hall on the corner of Castle Street and Waingate. The foundation stone of the new building was laid by Alderman W.J. Clegg in 1891 and the building was completed in 1896. The new Town Hall was opened by Queen Victoria on the 21st May 1897. It was designed by E.W. Mountford, the city architect, and is built of a warm fawn sandstone from the Stoke Hall Quarries in Derbyshire. The roofs are slated with green Westmorland slates and the turrets are of oak and copper. A statue of Queen Victoria stands on the Pinstone Street face in the centre gable. The front, on Pinstone Street, is rich in architectural detail and stone carving. There are two friezes, each 36 feet long, carved in stone depicting craftsmen such as smiths, grinders, smelters, miners, sculptors, workers in metal and ivory, painters and architects and includes a bulldog. Above the front arch are the Arms of Sheffield, supported by the gods Thor (Norse god of thunder) and Vulcan (Roman god of fire and metalworking).

On the tip of the 200ft tower stands an eight-foot-high bronze statue of Vulcan, a symbol of Sheffield's steel industry. He was placed there in December 1895. Vulcan's right foot is on an anvil, a hammer is in his right hand and pincers in his left.

The internal walls of the Town Hall are of a fine grain Coxbench stone which is suitable for carving. Inside the main entrance, the vestibule, hall, grand staircase and corridors are paved with marble and the walls lined with marble and alabaster. A statue, carved by Onslow Ford, of the 15th Duke of Norfolk stands at the bottom of the stairs, he was the first Lord Mayor of Sheffield. The Council Chamber and fine Reception Rooms have beautiful, decorated plaster ceilings and oak-panelled walls. The Lord Mayor's parlour has a handsome chimneypiece with an alabaster panel, depicting two figures holding the Shield of Faith and the Sword of the Spirit. Many portraits hang on the walls.

The Town Hall was extended in 1923 in a similar style and was opened by the Prince of Wales, later to become King Edward VIII. The 'egg box' (not listed) was added in 1977 to the south side, at a cost of £9 million. It was designed by the City Architects Department, headed by Bernard Warren and though, to many, the exterior is unimpressive, the interior gives a feeling of spaciousness and light. There are now plans to demolish this extension and the Peace Gardens are being reconstructed and will include the re-sited Goodwin Fountain.

The Cathedral Church of St Peter & St Paul

Church Street

Christians worshipped in Sheffield, probably on this site, from about 800 AD and the first building of which we have certain knowledge was built about 1100 AD. A perpendicular church was built here in the early 15th century to a cruciform plan with a central tower which still stands today, but this shape has been altered over the centuries by additions. In about 1520, during the reign of Henry VIII, the 4th Earl of Shrewsbury (Lord of the Manor) built a chapel, with a vault beneath, at the east end of the south choir aisle.

On the opposite side of the church, there was a wooden shed which housed the town's fire engine. In 1775 the Vicar and Church Burgesses petitioned the Duke of Norfolk to remove the fire engine shed to enable another addition 'to project equally with the Shrewsbury Chapel and thus make the East end of the Church beautiful and uniform'. So, in 1777, a vestry with a room above it was added.

By the end of the 18th century the Nave had become so dilapidated that it was decided that it should be demolished and rebuilt. This was achieved and reopened in 1805, but by 1880 more improvements and extensions were needed to meet the demands of this growing industrial town.

In 1913 a new diocese was formed and the Parish Church of Sheffield had conferred upon it the dignity of becoming a Cathedral.

The modern extension at the west end was built between 1963 and 1966, using stone quarried in Darley Dale, the new doors are full-length glass trimmed with stainless steel. In the roof of the modern part is a lantern of wood and glass which represents the crown of thorns. HRH Princess Margaret, Countess of Snowdon, attended the re-hallowing service on November 15th, 1966.

The church yard, once more extensive than the present, was last used for burials in 1855. The recent excavations of Church Street, for the track laying for Supertram in 1994, revealed bones that had to be removed and reburied. Since the completion of the Supertram works, the church yard has again been redesigned, replacing the grass with paving.

A booklet giving more detail of the Cathedral's history is available from the S.P.C.K. bookshop.

Abbeydale Works Museum

Abbeydale Industrial Hamlet, Abbeydale Road

The Abbeydale Works Museum, in Abbeydale Industrial Hamlet, has recently been uprated to Grade I. The Counting House and Workmen's Cottages are Grade II* as is the Manager's House and the adjoining stables on the east side.

The Hamlet was run by Sheffield City Museums and it has been preserved in much the same style as it would have been in the nineteenth century. Until recently it was open to the public and several 'working days' were held there each year, however, the site has now been 'mothballed' due to lack of funds. In November 1997 it was reported that some Sheffield steel and manufacturing companies had pledged £50,000 a year towards developing the City's industrial heritage museums, now in the hands of the newly formed Sheffield Industrial Museums Trust. In additon £55,000 has been promised by Sheffield City Council, and Meadowhall has given £25,000 to the project. It is hoped that the Hamlet will re-open this year.

The land originally belonged to the Premonstratensian monks of Beauchief Abbey who smelted lead, and sharpened scythes on water-powered grindstones. From 1782 to 1935 the Earls Fitzwilliam owned the land, during which time the Tilt Forge was developed. In the forge, blades were fashioned under a tilt hammer, which was driven by a water-wheel eighteen feet in diameter. The blades forged here were made from a high-quality steel, made from iron and a carbon flux heated together in clay pots called crucibles. After heating and skimming, the molten metal was poured into

Abbeydale Works Museum — blacking shop and warehouse

moulds and allowed to cool. If the ingot was satisfactory it was then reheated in the tilt forge and was hammered into the required shape. A steam engine was installed in 1855 to drive the tilt hammer. On working days various craftsmen could be seen making tools and instruments in the workshops.

The workmen's cottages and manager's house were built about 1880 and are furnished as they would have been in the 19th century. On working weekends they were occupied by ladies in period dress, serving in the cafe and baking bread. The warehouse contained an exhibition to explain the industrial workings, and there was also a shop where souvenirs and cards could be bought.

The crucible steel furnace shop

Fitting shop

Tilt hammer

Crucibles

Jessop tilt hammers from William Jessop's Brightside works

Grade II* Listed Buildings

Beauchief Abbey Remains

Church of St Thomas à Becket,
Beauchief Abbey Lane, Beauchief

Beauchief Abbey, together with its grounds, was presented to the City of Sheffield in 1931 by F. & F.M. Crawshaw. It was a Premonstratensian Abbey (a religious order started at Prémontré in Northern France in 1120) founded in about 1175 by Robert Fitz Ranulf, Lord of Alfreton. It is dedicated to Thomas à Becket. Examinations of the ruins suggest a nave 200ft long and 26ft wide, the tower which remains today would have been part of the western tower of the original building.

The monks of Beauchief held several services each day in the chapel, until the Dissolution of the Monasteries in 1536. After the dissolution, the extensive lands of the Beauchief estate were surrendered to the King, Henry VIII. In later times, the estate was held by the Lords of the Manor of Ecclesall, the Strelley Family. With the demise of the monastery the daily services also ceased.

In 1648, Gertrude Strelley, heiress to the estate of Ecclesall married Edward Pegge of Ashbourne. In 1662 Edward Pegge built the little church onto the tower of the ruin of the monastery. He also built a home, Beauchief Hall, near the Abbey, in 1671. In 1622 the vicar of Sheffield, Mr Toller, organised the restoration of the dilapidated walls and fitted it up for worship. They laid a floor in the chancel, set up pews, a pulpit and a communion table and glazed the windows. A small wooden steeple was erected.

Further restoration work was done in the nineteenth century. The interior of the church still has its complete furnishings of the seventeenth century, box pews, family pews for the squire and the rector, a pulpit in the south-east corner, reading desk and clerk's pew below, facing the altar table. There is a monument to Mrs E. Pegge-Burnell, 1844, a Gothic frame and relief of two figures illustrating charity.

The Abbey still stands in lovely surroundings, close by a golf course. Regular services are held at the church on Sundays.

Beauchief Hall
with Adjoining Steps, Forecourt Walls, and Gate
Beauchief Drive, off Abbey Lane

Eben-ezer.
Haec domus ergo Deus stet honoris grata columna:
Nam domus et domini conditor ipse Deus.
E.P. Maii 17, 1671

The above, as quoted by Joseph Hunter writing about 1819, is inscribed in stone over the entrance to Beauchief Hall. A suggested translation is: This house therefore stands to the honour of God: For God himself is the founder and Lord of the house. E.P. May 17th 1671.

The hall was built in 1671 by Edward Pegge, 1622–1679, High Sheriff of Derbyshire, using stone from the ruined abbey nearby. He became the owner of the estate through marriage in 1648 into the family of Sir Nicholas Strelley who had bought the Abbey Estate following the dissolution in 1537. Pegge's Cottage next to the hall, formerly described as a barn (Fairbanks), has a date stone over the door of 1667. The hall was altered in 1836 to its present form; a sturdy building on three floors. The most interesting external features are the wide stone steps going up to the main entrance on the first floor from the front garden, and the curved flights on each side leading down to the garden. The Latin inscription, with the date 1671, can be seen over the door. Higher still a stone, at roof level over the main entrance, bears the inscription 'BB PB 1836' said to stand for Broughton Benjamin Pegge-Burnell, the owner 1774–1850. Eight ornate rain hoppers have the same date. Interesting features inside are an alabaster fireplace depicting a gentleman in Tudor dress, which was originally in the dining room and is now in the entrance hall, given by Mr Adrian Mundy, of Quare, and some fine oak panelling. The corridors have red floor tiles, some with the arms of the Pegge-Burnell family.

The driveway as it is today was constructed some time before 1840. Previous access ran from the abbey across the present golf course and through the land to the rear, until recently used as a nursery garden by Sheffield City Council's Recreation Department, hence the gateway in front of the hall. A deer park and paddock used to be west of the hall.

The hall stayed in the Pegge-Burnell family until 1909 when it was rented to William Wilson, who then bought the hall in 1922. It has changed hands several times since then and was used as the De La Salle College for some years. It was restored in 1989 and is now the offices of a large electronic data processing company.

A 19th-century lady occupant of the hall was an avid pianist and, it is said, on quiet summer evenings she can still be heard playing her favourite pieces.

Based on research done by Rosamund Meredith 1967 and Tony Smith 1998

Bishops' House

Meersbrook Park, Norton Lees Lane

Bishops' House is the best preserved and earliest example of a timber-framed house in Sheffield. The first house, circa 1500, was completely framed in timber and consisted of an east wing, which held a hall open to the roof, with a kitchen adjoining, and a west wing in which were situated the family's private rooms. The present west wing is a mid-16th century replacement of the earlier wing. The second phase of improvements to the house came in the early 17th century, when fireplaces were installed in the parlour and the chamber above and new, larger windows were put into the rooms. Decorated plaster-work was added as a frieze over the fireplace of the chamber and a new ceiling put in the parlour. A floor was constructed over the hall to provide extra living space and wooden panelling affixed in the hall. The panelling is richly carved with strapwork motifs and the inscription 'WB 1627' is thought to stand for William Blythe, a commander in the Parliamentary Army in the Civil War. A partition wall was introduced between the hall and the parlour.

A stone extension was added to the north side of the west wing after 1642, two rooms with fireplaces, a cellar, and an improved staircase providing two-storey accommodation. The house was then let to a tenant farmer and his labourer in the mid-18th century and made into two separate dwellings.

According to Pauline Beswick:

> *The earliest occupant of the house for whom there is reasonable evidence is the William Blythe of 1627 whose initials appear on the panelling. From his will and inventory which survive in the Probate Registry of Lichfield, he was a farmer and perhaps the local producer of scythes before the Civil War. He died in 1631 leaving an estate of £641 (excluding debts), a wealthy and prosperous yeoman.*

In 1886, Sheffield Corporation bought Bishops' House with 37 acres of land and Meersbrook Hall for £7,500. It used the former dwelling as accommodation for the Recreation Department employees.

After extensive restoration the house was opened as a museum in July 1976. A leaflet, written by Pauline Beswick, giving more details of the history of Bishops' House is available from Sheffield City Museums. It is advisable to telephone before visiting as the opening hours are variable, 0114 255 7701.

Three Glasshouses

Botanical Gardens, Clarkhouse Road

The three glasshouses in the Botanical Gardens were designed by B.B. Taylor, the town's architect, and were built in 1837–38 to house exotic tropical plants. Each of the group of three conservatories is covered by a quadrangular dome, supported by metallic ribs built on buff-coloured Hathersage sandstone, they were originally linked by glazed colonnades to a total length of 100 yards. They were damaged during the Second World War but were since restored. In 1956 the small west pavilion was restored to its original design using, as far as possible, the original materials. Lowmoor iron was found and made up for the roof members. When, two years later, the central and east pavilions were restored, the supply of the original material was exhausted so modern alloys were used. The large central pavilion was converted into an aviary in 1960–61. In 1963–64 an aquarium was constructed in the small east pavilion.

The land for the gardens was bought from the Wilson family of Sharrow in 1833, by the Sheffield Botanical and Horticultural Society. The gardens occupy 18 acres of land and cost about £18,000 to establish in 1836. In the Victorian era, galas and promenades were held and music provided. Twenty to thirty thousand people were estimated to attend these functions, including the leading inhabitants of the town. Constant access was only permitted to the shareholders and subscribers and the gardens were open every day except Sunday mornings.

In 1898 the gardens were vested in the Town Trustees and maintained by the Sheffield Town Trust until 1951 when they were leased to Sheffield Corporation for future maintenance by the Parks Department. 1967 saw an educational centre established to provide demonstrations and lectures for the amateur gardener.

At the present time the pavilions are empty and in a dilapidated condition owing to the lack of funding from the City Council. However, in December 1997 it was reported that the Botanical Gardens will now be run by The Sheffield Botanical Gardens Trust, set up in September 1997, and The Friends of the Botanical Gardens. Fundraising for the renovations reached £7.5 million including a heritage lottery backed donation.

The first phase includes work on the gateway and the conversion of the curator's house into a falt and café. Refurbishment of the three glass houses is being planned.

Broom Hall

Broomhall Road

'This respectable old mansion stands a little to the north of the [river] Porter and about a mile west of Sheffield. It is a low building embosomed in trees: "secreta parentis Anchisae domus, arboribusque obtecta". Around it lay a beautiful estate richly cultivated, well watered, and well wooded.' So wrote Joseph Hunter around 1820. 'Part of it is of an age not later than the time of Henry VIII. The Jessops added to the original structure. The modern part was built by the Reverend James Wilkinson, Esq. Vicar of Sheffield, who resided in this hall of his maternal ancestors. He died in 1805.'

The first owners of Broom Hall, following the Dissolution of the Monasteries in the 15th century, appear to be the de Wickersley Family. In 1544, Robert and William Swift, of Rotherham, acquired large grants of Abbey land including a third of the Sheffield Tithes which had belonged to Worksop Priory (this included the right to nominate the Vicar of Sheffield Parish Church). Robert Swift was married to Ellen de Wickersley, heiress to Broom Hall. Their eldest daughter, Anne, who married Richard Jessop, inherited the estate, which is how the Jessop family came to Broom Hall and lived there for seven generations.

Francis Jessop, 1638–1691, was a JP, a Fellow of the Royal Society, an ornithologist, scientist and mathematician, a Church Burgess and Honorary Freeman of the Cutlers' Company. He also had an extensive library of science books. The hall eventually passed to his grandson, James Wilkinson, who was appointed the Vicar of Sheffield Parish Church, and Justice of the Peace, posts which he held for fifty years.

In 1791 Broom Hall was attacked by a mob of misguided and thoughtless people who set fire to the house and much damaged the library. The riots of 1791 were brought about as a result of the Enclosures Act which affected Crookes Common. James Wilkinson had little to do with the acts, but there was general disquiet at the administration of justice, and particularly unpopular was the widening of Church Street into the church yard and the disruption to the graveyard this caused. The mob, in search of a target for their anger, focused their attention on their Justice of the Peace, James Wilkinson.

After the death of James Wilkinson, in 1805, who had never married, the Hall passed to a cousin Philip Gell, (d.1841) the last of the Jessop line to inherit it. As he lived in Hopton, Derbyshire, he sold Broom Hall.

In the recent history of Broom Hall it was owned, in the 1960s, by the United Society for the Propagation of the Gospel, who wanted to pull down a third of the hall and build a six-storey office block!

In the 1970s and 1980s it was owned by the silversmith and industrial designer David Mellor and his wife, the writer Fiona MacCarthy. Then it was described as an Elizabethan manor house with a Georgian wing. It was in a state of considerable dilapidation and had been heavily vandalised when they acquired it in 1973. The Mellors set about restoring the property with the help of architects Mansell, Jenkinson & Partners, and in 1975 it won a Civic Trust Award in European Architectural Heritage Year. David Mellor set up his company, designing and making cutlery, in a studio workshop in the Georgian wing. Then the 15th-century wing was restored and became their home, affording a spacious and elegant setting for their collections of arts, crafts, antiques and paintings.

There is a legend that one room was haunted by a ghost which tapped on walls and trundled his own head about the fireplace. Since the conversion work carried out by David Mellor there have been no further sightings of the ghost.

In 1989 the Mellors moved to a new factory in Hathersage and Broom Hall was sold to the Omega Group plc, for £725,000, for use as offices for the property company. The hall now belongs to another property developer and is leased to the John Carlisle Partnership and to The Hallamshire Press, the publishers of this book.

15th-century wing before restoration (courtesy of David Mellor)

After restoration

Carbrook Hall

Attercliffe Common

The old timber-framed Carbrook Hall, built in 140 acres of meadow and woodland on Attercliffe Common, was the home of the Blunt family in 1176.

The present, stone, Carbrook Hall is thought to have been built by Stephen Bright in the reign of James I. The oak-panelled parlour was used for meetings of the Parliamentarian forces during the Civil War of 1642–1649. Later in the 17th century the Carbrook Estate belonged to Thomas Bright, who had brothers residing at Whirlow and Banner Cross. Hunter wrote (about 1810) 'The Hall at Carbrook has been deserted by its owners for more than a century but it still retains traces of its former consequence'. In 1819 the hall was bought by Thomas Booth & Company, they then sold it to George Bradford who owned a greater part of Attercliffe Common and land towards Tinsley. By 1855 the owners were the River Don Company and the tenants Carbrook Land Society, after which the hall deteriorated and became as described in *A Pub on Every Corner* 'a common beer-house'.

The best room in the house is the parlour, 22ft x 18ft, panelled in oak with the original door still hanging. The central feature is the carved wooden chimney piece in the wainscoted parlour. It shows the design of 'Wisdom trampling on Ignorance'. It depicts a nun who has fallen into disgrace. The Bishop standing over her symbolises her condemnation by the church. The inscriptions on the scrolls are:

Be not as horse and mule which have no understanding

Understanding reacheth heaven

Understanding is a well-spring of life

Good understandings depart from evil

Ignorance is a beast

In the early 19th century Hunter records that 'The Estate of Carbrook was sold to a building society and is now for the most part built upon'.

By the 20th century, Carbrook Hall was surrounded by factories relating to the steel industry but, since the recession of the 1980s, many of these buildings have been demolished and the public house then stood alone in a small paved area and garden.

Engraving by E. Blore

The 1990s brought much redevelopment in the Don Valley, changing the grime of the old steel industry, and the dilapidation that followed its decline, into modern buildings for light industry. Carbrook Hall now has a new life as a popular drinking place, serving sizzling meals to, amongst others, weary shoppers from Meadowhall. It claims to be the most haunted pub in Sheffield. A quote from the history leaflet available at the pub claims that John Bright, in Puritan dress, is one of several ghosts which haunt the hall. A Roundhead, in a black cap and tall white collar, has been seen behind the bar and in the doorway by the cigarette machine. In 1982 a new ghost was seen in the pool room, a monk-like figure in a hooded cloak. The old hall is said to have been built on the site of a monastery.

Carved chimney piece in oak panelled room

The City Hall

Barkers Pool

The City Hall in Barkers Pool, in the centre of Sheffield, was designed in 1920 by E. Vincent Harris and was built, in 1932, of Darley Dale stone in the twentieth-century Classical Revival style. The portico has eight giant Corinthian columns without pediment.

It was designed for concerts in the Oval Hall and meetings and dances in the ballroom below. The main auditorium, the Oval Hall, has great sweeping galleries and a platform for orchestral and choral concerts. The ceiling is decorated with rows of carved roses round a large oval skylight, unfortunately this is now partly obscured by the spotlight gantry.

The Grand Organ was built by Henry Willis & Sons Limited at a cost of £12,650. The specification was drawn up by the organ builder in consultation with Sir Edward Bairstow, then the organist of York Minster, who gave the opening recital in September 1932. This very large, four-manual concert organ of 75 speaking stops and 36 couplers (111 registers in all with over 3,500 pipes ranging from 32 feet in length to tiny one-inch-long pipes) is the only remaining example of its kind in the world built by Willis III, the grandson of Henry, still in an unaltered condition. To build such an instrument today would cost about one million pounds. The organ has recently (1994–1996) been revitalised, thanks to the hard work and dedication of the Sheffield and District Organists' & Choirmasters' Association (SADOCA) and the expert help of David Watson, the Sheffield organ-builder. Further restoration work still needs to be undertaken in the future.

Two, stone Assyrian Lions once guarded the centre stage of the Oval Hall but they were hated by visiting conductors who faced them during concerts, Sir Thomas Beecham was most vociferous about them. Eventually, in 1968, they were removed and acquired by Tarmac. Until recently they could be seen outside their offices in Matlock.

The ballroom below the main hall can accommodate 1,000 dancers. At the rear of the building is the semi-circular Memorial Hall which is used for smaller gatherings.

Memorial Hall

Cornish Place

East and West Range, Cornish Street

'Undoubtedly the most impressive cutlery factory that still stands in Sheffield...' according to Geoffrey Tweedale in *The Sheffield Knife Book*.

This very important piece of Sheffield's industrial heritage is located on about four acres of land by the river Don at Ball Bridge, near Kelham Island.

Cornish Place Works was the home of Messrs James Dixon and Sons, cutlery and sheet metal workers, a firm which was established in 1806. It was famous for the manufacture of a wide range of fine silverware and electro-plated goods but they also made objects in Britannia metal, which is a combination of block tin, copper, brass and martial regulus of antimony. Powder flasks and other shooting apparatus were manufactured as well as a wide range of cutlery. Dixon's won many awards for the excellence of their products and displayed examples of their work at the Great Exhibition of 1851 and the Paris Exhibition of 1855.

Cheap imports, the recession and the decline in the popularity of silverware hit firms such as Dixon's the hardest. Cornish Place Works was largely derelict at the end of the 1980s, yet in the firm's heyday they had employed 1,000 workers.

This derelict and dilapidated factory which, at the time of writing, is owned by a housing development firm, recently suffered a devastating fire.

The Cutlers' Hall

Church Street

The present Cutlers' Hall, the third on this site, (previous halls were built in 1638 and 1725) is a unique building dating from 1832, it was built at a cost of over £8,000. Designed by Samuel Worth and B.B. Taylor in a dignified Grecian style, it is one of the finest buildings in Yorkshire. It is the home of the Company of Cutlers in Hallamshire in the County of York, which was incorporated by act of Parliament in 1624 to regulate the cutlery trades of the area and to promote Sheffield and to protect 'Sheffield' as a Certified Trade Mark.

According to the Cutlers' Company, the first mention of the craft was in a tax return dated 1297, however, men were probably making cutting edges in Hallamshire well before that date but this is the first known use of the word 'cutler' in an official document. So, in 1997 the Company celebrated 700 years of craftsmanship in the industry.

In 1867, Sheffield architects, Flockton & Abbott added more grandeur to the building, with a spacious, branching, stone staircase with a cast-iron balustrade and ramped, scrolled, wooden handrail. They also designed the banqueting hall with a marbled, panelled, ladies' gallery at the north end, and on the east side, a three-arched moulded recess, the centre one having a bow-fronted, panelled gallery with a half dome.

The Cutlers' Hall, with its various public rooms, is an important venue for dinners and balls and other social occasions, including the prestigious Cutlers' Feast and the Forfeit Feast. It houses a magnificent collection of silver and cutlery of all types, including the renowned Norfolk Knife, a multi-bladed knife, over 2ft 6ins long when open, containing 75 various blades, tools and implements. The knife was made by the famous firm of Joseph Rodgers for the Great Exhibition of 1851. The blades are acid etched with various designs, such as the heads of the Royal Family and a view of Washington DC, and the pearl scales of the knife are beautifully carved with a hunting scene.

A line from Geoffrey Chaucer's *Canterbury Tales*, the 'Reeves Tale' is written around a frieze high up in the banqueting hall:

A Sheffeld thwitel [knife] *baar he in his hose.*

Also a quote from Ruskin declares:

In Cutlers' iron work we have in Sheffield the best of its kind, done by English hands unsurpassable when the workman chooses to do all he knows, by that of any living nation.

King Edward VII School

Glossop Road, Broomhill

This imposing building was designed, in 1838, in the Palladian style by William Flockton, it was thought to have cost the company of shareholders £14,500, including the spacious grounds. It was a Wesleyan College with accommodation for 250 boarders, with the Reverend Dr Waddy as the governor and chaplain. In 1906 it became the King Edward VII Grammar School for boys, following the amalgamation of the Wesleyan College with the Sheffield Royal Grammar School in Collegiate Crescent. At this time the Glossop Road building was extensively renovated. It is now a co-educational, comprehensive school, accommodating 1,540 day pupils and more than 90 teachers.

The present assembly hall has a curved gallery and there is an organ, in the elevated organ loft above the grand assembly hall, which was built by J.W. Walker and installed in 1950. It is a two manual extension organ with five ranks of pipes.

The director of music from 1947 to 1976, when he retired, was Norman J. Barnes MBE, MA, B Mus, FRCO, ARSCM. Many talented pupils passed through his department and have become professional musicians, scattered to the four corners of the world. The first organ student was Ivor H. Jones, who, at the time of writing, is the Master of Wesley House, Cambridge.

Set apart from the main building is a new suite of classrooms, music rooms and common rooms, imaginatively laid out in a curve. It was designed by DBS Architects, principal architect, Sue Williams. It was opened in September 1996 and has been entered for design awards.

Photograph by Aero Pictorial Ltd (c.1947)

Endcliffe Hall

Endcliffe Vale Road

The present Endcliffe Hall was built on the site of a previous house by one of Sheffield's wealthiest and most influential citizens, John Brown. Construction of the hall, stables, lodges and vinery started in 1863 and within two years the hall was occupied. The architects were Messrs T.J. Flockton & Abbott, the style of the hall is Italianate treated in the French manner. The outside of the stone porch is surmounted by stone figures, carved by E.W. Wyon, which represent the seasons. The reception vestibule has mosaic paving and a carved ceiling which originally was gilded. Leading off is a conservatory which contained a rockery, many plants and figures, and had a tessellated floor, large doors led to the garden terrace. The estimated cost of the building was £100,000 and a further £60,000 was spent on fittings and furnishings. 'The drawing rooms were stuffed full of the finest works of art that money could buy' reported John Tarn. In 1867 Queen Victoria 'was pleased to direct letters patent to be passed under the Great Seal granting the dignity of a Knight of the United Kingdom of Great Britain and Ireland unto John Brown of Endcliffe Hall...'

Sir John stayed at the house for nearly thirty years. His wife Mary died in 1881, they had no children and so, in 1892, he decided to sell the hall. No buyers were forthcoming and the estate was offered to Sheffield Corporation who replied after consideration that they were 'not prepared to entertain the proposal'. Sadly the break up of the estate became inevitable and the firm of Maple and Co. sold the contents at an auction which lasted five days. An elaborate catalogue was prepared, a copy of which is in the Brotherton Library at Leeds University.

The hall itself was then auctioned, along with 33 acres of land, in July 1895 and, after slow bidding, was bought for a mere £26,000 by Mr John Wortley acting on behalf of a syndicate of local businessmen, who eventually formed Endcliffe Estates Company, with the intent of developing the land for building purposes. In the meantime, the hall was used for dances, parties, fêtes and exhibitions but, by 1913, the company was wound up and there were plans to demolish the hall and redevelop the land. To the rescue came Colonel G.E. Branson, of the West Riding Territorial Force Association, with a suggestion that the hall should replace the old Hyde Park Barracks as the Hallamshires' headquarters and, on 26th January 1914, the purchase was completed. The hall has been used by the T.A.V.R. ever since.

A booklet containing further history, and pictures of the interior when sumptuously furnished, written by D. Hindmarsh and A.J. Podmore is available from the T.A.V.R. at Endcliffe Hall, Endcliffe Vale Road.

The Gas Offices

Commercial Street

The Gas Offices, now known as Canada House, were designed for the Sheffield United Gas Light Company by M.E. Hadfield & Son of Sheffield and were built in 1874 in the classical style of a grand Italian villa. Inside are important plaster covings and ceilings and period fireplaces. The General Office contains a glazed dome by J.F. Bentley and there are art works by Earp and Stannus. Two figures adorn the main entrance, and there are columns of pink granite on the front facade. Improvements and additions were made in 1890.

The Gas Board moved to new premises in 1972 and the building was offered for sale but no buyers were forthcoming. Permission was sought to demolish the building and redevelop the site, but several preservation societies objected and the building remained. An inquiry was held in 1977, the Assistant Chief Planner for Sheffield, David Cathels, said the building was considered to be 'a vigorous and distinguished example of Victorian architecture which should be retained'.

In 1978 a local businessman, Les Vickers, paid £110,000 for the offices which he planned to make into an hotel and conference centre but this did not happen and it was used as a night club for several years. In 1990 Canadian Business Parks of Bedfordshire took over with plans for restorations but had financial difficulties and the building has remained empty and continues to deteriorate.

In January 1996 Sheffield City Council served legal notices on the owners to effect repairs but to no avail. Rain poured in through vandalised roofs and the period fireplaces were stripped out by thieves. The Council and English Heritage have a rescue plan to seal the building against the weather and protect it from further vandalism. The building has been acquired by English Partnerships, the Government agency for regeneration. The present plan is to convert it into an hotel, or bar, restaurant and offices.

Main entrance

Green Lane Works' Gateway

Green Lane, Shalesmoor

Green Lane Works were established in 1795 by Henry Hoole and Thomas Nicholson. The complex consisted of workshops, a counting house, a warehouse, a steam-engine house and cottages, the company was involved in the manufacture of stove grates, fenders and fire irons, and iron candlesticks. Hoole and Nicholson were merchants, steel converters and iron and brass founders. In 1842 Nicholson left the business but Hoole continued to flourish and, in 1860, had the splendid gateway entrance constructed. The stone arch with clock tower above, and the relief panels of Vulcan to one side and the Arts on the other side of the main entrance was designed by sculptor and artist, Alfred Stevens. Hoole and Company ceased to trade in 1933 and the property was occupied by A. Scott, a wholesale upholstery manufacturer, followed by W.A. Tyzack, a light engineering firm.

Several applications to demolish the works and redevelop the site have been made but were contested by the Hallamshire Historic Buildings Society on the grounds that the complex was visually interesting and of artistic importance to Sheffield's industrial heritage. The applications were withdrawn.

Some dilapidation of the gateway and exterior of the works had occurred so, in 1985, under the guidance of Neville Slack and Company and financed by the South Yorkshire Council and the Historic Buildings Council, they were restored.

Royal Infirmary

Heritage House, Infirmary Road

The General Infirmary, granted Royal status by Queen Victoria, was designed by John Rawsthorne and built in stone, between 1793 and 1797, with money raised by public subscription at the instigation of a Doctor Browne. Two sculptured figures, representing 'Hope' and 'Charity' still stand at each side of the main door. They are early works of Francis Chantrey of Norton. Inside, at each end of the front corridor, are round stairwells with cantilever, oval, winder, stone stairs complete with iron, stick balusters and ramped, scrolled handrails.

Other parts of the complex, such as the Round House, which was an outpatients hall, and Centenary House, which was the nurses home, are listed Grade II.

The south-east wing of the centre block was accommodation for nurses and was said to be haunted by the Grey Lady who silently walked the corridors at night. However, the Senior Night Sister at one time was a buxom woman who wore a grey uniform dress and a starched frilly cap with a white bow under her chin. At 2am she went from bed to bed and ward to ward checking the patients; timid, half-asleep nurses could be excused for thinking that she was the ghost.

Hope

Charity

The Royal Infirmary closed in 1980 having been superseded by the new Hallamshire Hospital in the 1970s. The complex was taken over by a property developer and it lay in a state of increasing dereliction and suffered from vandalism for some years. In 1990 the Norwich Union moved their insurance and financial services to the site which was renamed as the Heritage Park Development. The Surgical block was replaced by a modern supermarket building which does not reflect the former grandeur of the 18th-century buildings. 1998 sees the building once again empty and to let.

The Lyceum Theatre

Tudor Square

The City Theatre was opened in December, 1893, on the site of a wooden structure of 1879, called Alexander Stacey's Circus, which had been destroyed by fire. The new City Theatre was renamed the Lyceum in January 1897. It was built to a design by W.G.R. Sprague, a leading theatre designer who worked on many London theatres including the Aldwych, Ambassadors, The Strand and Wyndham's. The Lyceum is said to be the only surviving theatre designed by Sprague outside London. It attracted many famous names including Sir Henry Irving, Charlie Chaplin, Ellen Terry and the D'Oyly Carte. During the '50s and '60s successful pantomimes ran for several months starring, for example, Jewel and Warris, and Morcambe and Wise, but under-investment in refurbishment by the owners, the Beaumont family, led to a steady decline and it closed as a theatre in 1968.

In 1972, the Lyceum was listed Grade II because of its splendid Rococo plasterwork. 1974 saw it being used as a bingo hall and there were plans to demolish it and build an arts–leisure centre on the site but the Secretary of State refused permission. In 1975 the Lyceum Trust was formed to campaign for its retention and refurbishment, as it was the only remaining theatre out of eight previous ones that were operational in

Sheffield in the 19th century. In July 1981 the Lyceum was sold to two club owners who were to use it for pop concerts. 1982 saw it for sale again. In 1985 planning permission was sought to make it into a discotheque. These plans were rejected and the building was 'mothballed' whilst restoration plans were made. The Lyceum was Grade II* listed to enable further funding to be raised.

Twelve million pounds were spent on the renovation bringing it to its present delightful condition. The auditorium is virtually a true replica of the original design with a three tier, horseshoe-shaped, auditorium avoiding the use of pillars which would obstruct the view from some seats. The seating provides for 1,130 people and the stage is one of the deepest in the country. Modern facilities have been provided both back-stage and in the dressing rooms. Consultant, Clare Ferraby, took samples of plaster mouldings, paint and gold leaf to match the original interior decor. The paintings above the boxes,  which had not survived, have been designed in the romantic classical style. It was reopened in December, 1990, and is now a very popular venue for visiting theatre companies.

The Mappin Art Gallery

Weston Park

Weston House, originally set in thirteen acres of parkland, was last used as a dwelling by two sisters, Eliza and Anne Harrison, who were great benefactors. Their father, Thomas Harrison, had been a saw maker at Hollins Croft. In 1873, after their demise, the house and land were acquired by Sheffield Corporation and Weston Park was available to be enjoyed by the public. In 1875, Weston House became a museum to house several donated collections, such as cutlery, pottery, prehistoric antiquities and archaeological artefacts.

In 1887, John Newton Mappin bequeathed his extensive collection of paintings, said to have been to the value of over £80,000, to the Town of Sheffield. An art gallery was needed to accommodate them.

Sheffield architects, Flockton & Gibbs were chosen to design the gallery. They chose a Greek Revival style for the building which is fronted by an Ionic portico, with a pediment topped with a lion, and an Ionic colonnade at each side. It was completed in 1888 at a cost of £15,000. The Weston House Museum needed more space for its growing collection and a new purpose-built museum was created to link with the Mappin Art Gallery. The whole project was funded by Alderman J.G. Graves.

Further extensions were built between 1961 and 1965, designed by city architect, J.L. Womersley. Although the original Weston House does not exist now, the grand classical building stands proudly in the park. The collections inside include Sheffield silver, Sheffield Plate, cutlery, pottery, archaeological and natural history artefacts.

The Mount

Glossop Road, Broomhill

One of the finest developments in Broomhill was The Mount, an impressive Palladian mansion comprising eight 'genteel dwellings' designed by William Flockton in the 1830s. The residences were numbered 2–16 from the Newbold Lane end towards Glossop Road.

No. 2. Walton J. Hadfield, the city surveyor, lived here from 1926 to 1934.

No. 4. James Montgomery, the poet, lived at No. 4 with the two Misses Gale, spinster daughters of the proprietor of the *Register* newspaper, which later became the *Iris* when Montgomery was in sole charge. He lived there until his death, in 1854, aged 82 years.

No. 6. Occupied from 1837 to 1862 by James Wilkinson, a merchant in iron and steel, his widow Elizabeth stayed until 1883. From 1934 to 1938 John Rothenstein, the director of the Graves Art Gallery, lived there, followed by Geoffrey Ost, the producer at the Playhouse.

No. 8. The home, from 1837 until 1841, of George Wostenholm, the famous cutlery manufacturer. He was followed by Thomas W. Rodgers, the registrar for Sheffield, who lived there till 1862. The next occupant was Frederick Fowler, a civil engineer and County Court Surveyor, the brother of Sir John Fowler, the civil engineer who worked on designs for the Forth Bridge and the Wicker Arches.

No. 10. Sir James Arnold Knight was its first inhabitant until 1841. Sir James was a medical doctor and was one of the first to recognise 'grinder's lung disease'. He was the founder of the Dispensary, which later became the Royal Hospital, and he was the first commoner in Sheffield to be Knighted. William Parkin of Parkin & Marshall lived at No. 10 from 1881 until 1914.

No. 12. No distinguished residents lived here, but 14 and 16 were lived in by George Wilson, the snuff manufacturer, from 1857 until 1867, one house was not big enough for his family!

In 1914 when John Walsh's store took over Nos. 10–16 as housing for their staff, 'the tone of the residents went down' according to William Parkin, a former resident.

During World War II, Walsh's department store, which had been bombed at its High Street premises, continued trading from The Mount until their store was rebuilt in 1965. Now The Mount is owned by the General Accident Insurance Company, their property includes a large office block behind the Flockton Building and a covered car park which, unfortunately, obstructs the view of the elegant Palladian facade when viewed from the road.

Research by Eva Wilkinson.

Mount Pleasant
and Former Stables and Coach House

3, Sharrow Lane

This three-storey, brick house was designed and built by John Platt in 1777 for Francis Hurt who, in 1738, had changed his name to Sitwell in order to inherit his uncle's Renishaw Estate. He used Mount Pleasant as a second home for many years.

John Platt was a Rotherham architect, his biographer described Mount Pleasant as being 'the best example of its age and period in Sheffield'. After Sitwell, several wealthy tradesmen owned the house until, in 1868, the trustees let it to the West Riding authorities to serve as a temporary, pauper lunatic asylum. When it was eventually sold, it became a girls' Charity School from 1872 until 1939. In 1948 the Corporation of Sheffield bought it and the building was let, first to the Coal Board and then as Government Offices.

At present the building is used as an adult education and community centre. Its elegant exterior belies its spartan interior.

Further details of the house can be found in *A History of the Parish of St Barnabas, Highfield, Sheffield* by Mary Walton and Gerald R. Mettam.

Stable block

Norton Hall

with Colonnade and Orangery

Norton Church Road

Norton Hall was described in *The History of Chesterfield*, by the Reverend George Hall as:

> One of those picturesque old mansions of our country gentry of the high order, of which so few remain. Some portions of it were of very high antiquity. There was a fine entrance hall and in this, the non-conformists of Norton and the neighbourhood were accustomed to assemble for public worship.

Sadly, he was describing a previous building on this site, for Samuel Shore, a banker, built the present hall in 1815. This is probably the third house on the site.

Norton Hall was the family home of a well-respected long line of the Shore family, of which Florence Nightingale is the most famous. The new hall was described as a fine mansion with a spacious park, but Francis Chantrey, the famous sculptor born in Norton, described it as a 'Packing-box with windows in'.

When Shore's Bank in Church Street failed in 1850, the estate was sold at auction to Charles Cammell of the Cyclops Steel Works (steel rolling mills). The auction catalogue described the hall and park as featuring 'The entrance, supported by four columns, a private chapel near the hall, a gamekeeper's house, great oak trees, about 200 acres of park and woodland, sheets of water and a walled garden of one acre and a half'. Cammell added a grand dining-room, a billiard room and a colonnade. A later owner, in 1902, was Mr. Bernard Alexander Firth, who was a son of Mark Firth, the well known steel manufacturer and benefactor. He had the dining room panelled in oak after which it became known as the Oak Room. It has a 17th-century marble fireplace.

The grounds of Norton Hall, incorporated into Graves Park, were given to the town to serve as a lung for the Sheffield people. The park forms part of the ten-mile Round Walk.

For many years the hall was the Norton Annexe of the Jessop Hospital for Women, then it passed from the National Health Service and became a private clinic. At the time of writing the hall is unoccupied. The Stable Block adjoining Bunting Nook was converted into private residential accommodation.

Stable block before conversion

Norton Hall

Trademan's entrance

Oakes Park

and adjoining Terrace Wall and Steps and Gateway
and adjoining Walls at Garden Entrance to Oakes Park

Norton Lane

The Oakes in Norton is a large, 17th-century country house refitted and extended and latterly re-fronted in the 19th century. Its accommodation includes five reception rooms, service rooms and kitchen, two principle staircases, seven first floor bedrooms, five second floor bedrooms, four bathrooms and other living rooms.

The present mansion was probably built about 1668 by John Lee of Hazelbarrow for his bride, Barbara. Unfortunately she died in the same year, so John Lee sold it to Francis Barker of Lees Hall in 1672. Then the house changed hands several times until, in 1681, Henry Gill of Rotherham and Elizabeth Westby bought it. Henry's eldest daughter, Elizabeth, married Richard Bagshawe in 1699. He was the second son of Adam Bagshawe of Wormhill. The Oakes has been the home of the Bagshawe family from that time until recently.

The original house was altered in the 19th century by Sir William Chambers Bagshawe, who also redesigned the land. Napoleonic War prisoners helped to dig out a lake, a walled garden was constructed and over 100 acres were enclosed as a park. The terrace in front of the house was designed by Sir Francis Chantrey, the sculptor born in Norton, and the flower beds and garden were reputedly designed by John Nash, the architect of Buckingham Palace.

When Major Thornber Bagshawe came to the house in 1961 there was no electric lighting, telephone or other modern amenities. He, and his wife Hilary, spent a considerable amount of time and money restoring the house and opened it to the public as Sheffield's little stately home. The demise of the house came when an outer ring road was constructed around the city which divided the estate in two. Many old buildings and two cruck barns were demolished.

Amongst the treasures of The Oakes are the beautiful iron gates. They were made of metal obtained from the estate, and cast probably at Delve's Wood where evidence of mining operations was still present in 1910. The larger gates bear the arms of the Bagshawe family, and the smaller gates have the initials of Richard Bagshawe.

The Bagshawes moved away and The Oakes and the Park were bought by Henry Boot, property developers. The house, which appears to be empty, is now in private ownership and visitors are not encouraged.

Entrance gates

Old Bank House

3, Hartshead

Old Bank House was built in 1728 by a merchant, Nicholas Broadbent, in Hartshead Square. (Hartshead was a name given to a piece of land to the east of a church and from a religious practice of hanging the head of a male deer over a doorway.)

It is a three-storey brick building, when first built, the house was surrounded by gardens with an avenue leading from York Street. There are vaulted cellars beneath Bank House, said to be twenty feet below road level. Some rooms are panelled in wood and have grand fireplaces and ornate plaster ceilings. The remains of a crane are evident in the attic, a relic of merchant activities.

The water drain has the initials N.R.B. (Nicholas and Rebecca Broadbent) and the date at the top. Thomas Broadbent, a grandson of Nicholas, founded a private bank in the house in 1771, hence its name, but this bank only lasted until 1782.

Heavy development in later decades, such as St Peter's Close through the archway on the left, caused this area of Sheffield to become densely populated. However, in 1924 many buildings on Campo Lane were demolished for road widening.

Old Bank House was renovated in 1978 and is now used as offices.

Old Queen's Head Public House

40, Pond Hill

The 'Hawl in the Ponds' is said to be the oldest existing building in Sheffield. It is thought to have been built by the 4th Earl of Shrewsbury in the 15th century, circa 1475, for use as a hunting lodge to Sheffield Castle. It stood in a marshy, flat area by the River Sheaf, a garden on the north side extended down to the river where the nobility fished and shot wildfowl.

An account dated 1770 describes it as a 'former wash house to the Sheffield Manor'. In 1841 James Pilley, a nail and rivet maker, bought a two guinea licence to use it as a beer-house. As trade increased, a victualler's licence was obtained and the building was named the *Old Queen's Head*. The public house was described as consisting of one bar, one bar parlour, one tap room, a kitchen and three bedrooms. By 1884 the brewer Thomas Berry was the owner and it was eventually passed to Tennant Brothers brewery, now part of the Whitbread Group. In 1935, the public house was taken over by the Sheffield Corporation who leased it to John Smith's Brewery of Tadcaster.

Extensive restoration was done in 1949, when the timber frame and carvings were revealed by removing many layers of plaster and whitewash. An old stone fireplace and two mullion windows were uncovered inside the building and a well was found when workmen were digging for a cellar.

On this timber-framed building there are two carved heads on the external frontage said to represent the Sixth Earl of Shrewsbury, keeper of the Manor, and Bess of Hardwick.

This building has had a chequered career over the centuries. Old drawings and photographs show severe dilapidation at some times and at others restoration in different styles. Recently, however, 1992–93, it has been restored again and extended to facilitate the serving of meals. At present it is run by the Tom Cobleigh group, but the building is owned by the South Yorkshire Passenger Transport Executive who run the Pond Street bus station which occupies the adjoining land.

Etching by W. Hughes

*Carved heads by
the door*

Paradise Square

Nos. 1-15, 17, 19, 4-12, 14-22 and 24

Paradise Square has been described as the most elegant part of the city centre. In 1736, Thomas Broadbent, also associated with No. 3 Hartshead, laid out the first part of Paradise Square on the east side, on what was then a cornfield owned by the Trustees of the Shrewsbury Hospital. Development of the square continued, on the fields and orchards, mainly in an Anglo-Palladian style, to house the wealthier Georgian middle classes.

Famous occupants of the square include Francis Chantrey, the famous sculptor from Norton, who had a studio in the north-west corner in 1802. Here he drew portraits and miniatures in crayons which he sold for two to three guineas each. Dr David Daniel Davis, a physician who attended the birth of Queen Victoria in 1819, had a house on the east side.

There are reports of one John Lees who, in 1796, sold his wife at a public auction in the square, after she had been driven there like a horse with a halter around her neck. Apparently this was the customary way of getting rid of an unwanted wife in the 18th century!

The steeply sloping ground made it a grand arena for public speaking. Crowds of 20,000 are reported to have filled the cobbled area. The most famous speaker was the preacher John Wesley who, in 1779, stood on steps on the south side to address the largest crowd he had seen on a weekday. A plaque on the building informs us of this occasion.

Apart from the cars parked on the cobbles, the square has retained much of its original appearance, though instead of providing housing for the wealthy gentlemen of Sheffield, the buildings are used as offices for solicitors and other professionals.

The grandest house is No. 18, on the lower side, which has had various uses including, a Masonic lodge, a private school and an office of the Automobile Association when it became known as Fanum House.

Sheffield City libraries have published a book *The Story of Paradise Square* by Alan Hall and Alice Walton.

Paradise Square — south-west corner

Paradise Square — north-west corner

Sanderson Kayser

Two Workshops

Darnall Road

The most surprising location for a Grade II* listed building is in a steel works and yet it is this very industry that made Sheffield a great city hence the reason for its listing.

The crucible shops are tucked away in the south-east corner of the Darnall Road Works and are therefore not available for general visiting, though the management is very obliging. The five crucible steel making shops, now used as stores, date back to 1872. They have crucible furnaces inside and iron brackets for crucible-drying shelves and for tools. On the south-west side of the works is another small crucible steel shop.

Before Sanderson and Kayser joined together in 1960 they were the well known Sheffield firms of, Sanderson Brothers and Newbould Limited; established in 1776, and Kayser Ellison & Co. Limited; established in 1825, both were manufacturers of special steels. In addition to steel, Sandersons made saws and machine knives and Kayser Ellison developed bright steel and wires.

Sanderson Brothers and Co. developed a melting works at Darnall Road in 1835. They pioneered the development of high speed and other alloy tool steels, first by crucible, then later by electric melting. Their specialities included machine knives, saws, engineers' tools and high-ratio speed reducing gear.

C.W. Kayser (died 1947) started a plant in Darnall in 1913 with electric arc furnaces and pneumatic hammers. They took over the Darnall crucible plant from Sanderson Brothers and Newbould in 1934, but the crucible became less important as Kayser's extended their facilities for electric arc and high frequency induction melting, though some crucible steel was made during the war.

Crucible shops

Industrial remains at the Darnall Road site

Interior of crucible shop

Sharrow Snuff Mills

Ecclesall Road

This old building at Sharrow is the world's oldest snuff mill. The Mill House belonged to the Duke of Norfolk who, in 1737, rented the water-wheel and buildings to Thomas Wilson, the first of a long line of Wilsons to be associated with the property. His son, Joseph, was a silversmith who was associated with Thomas Boulsover, the inventor of Sheffield Plate. He continued to make scythes and shears at Sharrow until, in the 1740s, he came upon the secret formula for making snuff and in the next decade snuff manufacturing became the main industry.

Snuff, a finely powdered tobacco of various blends and flavours, which is sniffed into the nostrils, became popular with the English aristocracy in the eighteenth century, though it had been popular with the French and Scots at an earlier period. A Scots Highlander in a kilt was the sign used to denote that a shop sold snuff.

Six further generations of the Wilson Family followed Joseph, and the business, Wilson & Co. (Sharrow), is still wholly owned and run by the Wilson family.

Originally the power to drive the iron pestles in elm mortars, each weighing about two hundredweights, which grind bunches of dried tobacco leaves imported from Asia and North America, was provided by a water-wheel fed by the River Porter. In 1797 steam power was introduced, though the water-wheel is still in working order. The powdered tobacco is aged in oak barrels, then blended with herbs and oils.

The figure of a Scots Highlander stands with two oak barrels by the low, and very wide, ancient door.

The Scots Highlander

Old oak barrels

Iron pestels in elm mortars grinding dried tobacco leaves

Shepherd Wheel
and Attached Dam, Goyt and Weir
off Hangingwater Road

Shepherd Wheel, situated on the River Porter at Hangingwater Road, has two old grinding hulls (workshops). The wheel is thought to be the one mentioned in the will of Roger Barnsley dated 1566, then called 'Potar Whele'. It became known as Shepherd Wheel because Edward Shepherd was a tenant in the eighteenth century. In 1794 he employed ten men, occupying ten troughs. The ten men would work independently, making their own bundle of knives.

The present interior has, in the main hull, a cast-iron spur wheel which drives five grindstones with a shaft and belt connecting to four similar grindstones in the small hull. The machinery is complete and in working order.

The working life of the hull ended in the 1930s, thereafter it fell into dereliction. In 1957, £500 was allocated by the City Council for the demolition of the workshop, but the Council for the Conservation of Sheffield Antiquities persuaded the City Council to spend that money on the restoration of the building and the conservation group undertook the task of repairing the wheel and machinery, this was done with the help of grants from local industries. Further restoration was carried out in 1972. At the time of writing Shepherd Wheel is closed to the public due to lack of funds.

The workshops

The water wheel

The Church of St James the Great

Norton Church Road, Norton

Norton church is a typically English, stone perpendicular building of modest proportions, the interior of which gives one a cosy feeling of antiquity. It dates back to about 1183, when the Lord of the Manor, Robert Fitzranulf, bestowed the church to Beauchief Abbey. Changes have been made to the Norman church almost every century since.

The oldest part is thought to be the porch, with its zigzag Norman archway over the heavy wooden door, this was sensitively restored in 1882. Old gravestones which were once inside the church now line the porch walls. One of these commemorates the death of Barbara Lee, in 1670 at the age of 28, it is said that she is buried in an upright position near the altar. Another mentions William Blythe of Bishops' House and others are to William Scriven and Nicholas Stones, who were local benefactors.

In the baptistry is an ancient, carved-stone octagonal font dating from 1220. Near to the font is an old clapper from a tenor bell which came from Beauchief Abbey at the dissolution of the monasteries, the clapper was at one time used as a doorstop. The bell tower contains eight bells, the present tenor bell weighs over 15cwts.

There are lovely 19th-century stained glass windows depicting biblical scenes, and a plaster-cast statue of Sir Francis Chantrey sits in the north aisle.

The 1876 organ, built by Brindley and Foster of Sheffield, has twice been rebuilt, it has also been relocated and electrified. It has two manuals and a pedal organ and over 1,200 speaking pipes.

The Blythe Chapel, on the south side, was newly built in 1524, dedicated to St Katherin and endowed by the Bishop of Lichfield, Geoffrey Blythe. The oak roof contains the original carved bosses.

The graveyard was used, until 1869, as a burial ground for a large area of north Derbyshire. The famous sculptor, Sir Francis Chantrey of Norton, lies in a grave surrounded by railings near to the porch.

As St James is locked when not in use, the best time to visit is before or after a Sunday service, or, on a Wednesday morning when Communion is at 10am. A booklet on the church, written by the Norton History Group, is available there, price £1.

The Church of St John the Evangelist

Ranmoor

The church was first built in 1879, from a design by the Sheffield architect, E.M. Gibbs, and was described as Gothic of the early English style. Unfortunately, that first building caught fire in its tenth year and all except the tower and its spire were lost. It happened on new year's eve, when the country was in the grip of a severe frost. The following day being a Sunday, the Verger kept a big fire burning in the stove all night. According to the 75th Anniversary Booklet of 1954, 'He was in church early in the morning and at 8.30 went home for breakfast'. On returning to church at 9.20 he found the organ on fire. 'Leighton hastened to Ranmoor Inn, and a messenger was despatched on horse-back to Broomhill Police Station, whence a telephone message was sent to the Sheffield Fire Station; but before the fire-engine could be on the spot, the flames had got the mastery, and running up the organ screen, quickly set fire to the roof'. 'The roof fell in and the Nave was a vast furnace, the flames and smoke from which were seen from the hills of Ecclesall, Sharrow, and Crookes…and Fulwood'. 'The tower and spire…were saved by the courageous action of Superintendent Pound, who made his way up the spiral staircase to the Belfry taking a hose pipe with him.'

The church was rebuilt in twenty months to a new design by the same architect, E.M. Gibbs, in partnership with T.J. Flockton, the new style being described as Gothic of the Decorated period. The church is built of Ancaster stone, the sanctuary and choir floors are marble. The reredos, depicting the last supper, with St Peter and St Paul at each end, is carved from alabaster, it was done by Frank Tory who also carved the deeply undercut mouldings and rich capitals. A challenge was issued to the choirboys one year recently, to count the carved heads both in wood and in stone; they found over one hundred!

The spire rises to 200ft and is visible from many parts of Sheffield. The tower houses the belfry with ten bells. A feature of the interior is the Triforium, access to which is via a spiral staircase in one of the pillars of the nave. There is a small Lady Chapel in the south transept and the three manual organ with 3,000 pipes, built by Brindley and Foster, occupies the north transept. There are many fine stained glass windows.

The interior of the church was reordered in 1990–93 at the instigation of the vicar, the Reverend Michael Jarratt, under the guidance of the architect, Mr R. Simms, who also worked on the Cathedrals of Southwark, Southwell, Newcastle and Carlisle. The plan was to create a central altar, whilst retaining the original high altar, to bring the sacrament closer to the communicants. The timbers at the east end were to be lightened, bleaching the wood to the colour of stone, and the roof bosses were to be gilded. A new stone altar was to be placed in the chapel. The west-end doors were to be draught-proofed, the lighting redesigned, the floor was to be paved and new wooden furniture was to be introduced. More controversially, metalwork candle holders and a processional cross with a crown of thorns were planned, along with a redesigned font cover. These changes were not favoured by the Victorian Society, who contested the plans on the grounds that the fine Victorian church should be left intact for future generations to appreciate and enjoy. A consistory court was held and some modifications were made to the original plans. The rest of the work was done.

In 1997 the organ was rebuilt. In spite of the recent changes, St John's is surely still the finest parish church in Sheffield.

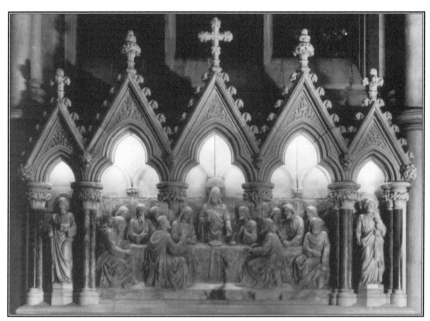

The reredos depicting The Last Supper

St Mary's

Bramall Lane

In the early 19th century, the established church was lagging behind in providing places of worship for the populations migrating to the towns to work in industry. In 1800 the parish of Sheffield had a population of 45,758 but the Church of England had sittings for only 3,600 worshippers. In 1818, Lord Liverpool, heading the Tory government, was instrumental in providing one million pounds from public funds (this was eventually increased by another half million) to be spent on the provision of churches, this was the Church Building Act, better known as 'the million pound fund'. Sheffield built four churches: St George's, Broad Lane, consecrated in 1825; Christ Church, Attercliffe, in 1826, now demolished; St Philip's near the Royal Infirmary, in 1928, now demolished; and St Mary's, Bramall Lane, in 1830, the only one still used for worship.

Three acres of land were given by the Duke of Norfolk, whose estate still includes many properties in the area, for the new church which was to stand at the edge of the town. It was surrounded by fields and gardens, through which flowed the River Sheaf, stretching out to Norfolk Park and to the hamlet of Heeley.

The foundation stone was laid in Bramall Lane on October 12th 1826 by the Countess of Surrey. Also present were Earl Fitzwilliam, the Earl of Surrey and Lord Wharncliffe, and a large company of townsmen. The building cost £12,649 19s. 5d. defrayed out of the million pound fund. The church took four years to build and was consecrated on July 21st 1830. It provided 2,000 seats, 800 of which were free. Originally it was a Chapel of Ease to the Parish Church, consequently there were no marriages performed there until 1846 when it became a separate parish. In 1831 the Town Trustees contributed £20 towards a clock and a bell then, in 1867, a new clock costing £230, was fixed in the tower.

The organ, built by William Hill, was purchased by public subscription in 1853 and placed in the west-end gallery, it was extended in 1876. The interior of the church was rearranged in 1888 reducing the number of seats to 1,550. The organ was redesigned by Brindley and Foster, the Sheffield firm of organ builders, and relocated into the east bay of the north aisle; new choir stalls were introduced and a choir vestry made on the south side. In November 1839, during the Chartists' agitation, an attempt was made to set fire to the church by throwing in balls of combustible matter. Happily, the fuses became separated and so the plot failed.

Although the million pound fund churches were intended for the impoverished industrial workers, St Mary's congregation consisted of the urban middle classes, artisans, new owners of industry and their professional colleagues—solicitors, magistrates, brewers, doctors and merchants—whose mansions had spread to the south and east of the town.

There are reports from 1870 of an average congregation of 1,000 in the body of the church and 400 in the galleries. The Reverend Robert Henry Hammond, vicar from 1893–1902, had 700 people in his bible classes on Sunday afternoons.

Alas, during World War II, on the night of December 12th 1940, the church was blasted and the roof laid open to the winter weather. Because of the war, repairs were not possible and it soon became unsafe for worship. It was not until 1954 that the final plans were drawn up for rebuilding but, because of the changes in the ever-expanding City and the movement of residents spreading further afield, it was decided to split the long nave in half. This north-south partition left the west end of the building serving as a secular, independent, community centre. The ceiling was lowered to give better proportions to the shortened nave, so parts of the original groined and ribbed roof that survived the blitz are hidden in the void above the ceiling. The new building was officially re-opened on 13th March 1957, with HRH Princess Alexandra as guest of honour.

The building of the ring road in 1978 took away half of the north side grave-yard. The bodies were re-interred in other burial grounds, the area around the church was landscaped and paved with many of the old gravestones, and the gates at the former main entrance were re-located to their present position. In 1980 the church was sand-blasted to remove the old industrial grime, it took 50 tons of sand and cost £13,900—more than the original cost of building the church.

The motto of the church is:

Attempt great things for God
Expect great things from God

St Mary's pre-1940 (courtesy of St Mary's)

The Church of St Mary the Virgin

High Street, Beighton

Beighton was an Anglo-Saxon settlement which was mentioned in the Domesday Book, and although the church was not mentioned at that time it is not surprising that this ancient parish has a very old church. The origins of St Mary's church, based on the discovery of a crumbling late-Norman chancel arch in 1867, date back to the 12th century, with additions in the 14th and 15th centuries. It was restored in 1773 and 1867. Formerly, Beighton was in Derbyshire but since the boundary changes, in 1967, the county of South Yorkshire and the City of Sheffield have taken the area into their jurisdiction.

The church is first mentioned in an undated deed, written in the reign of Edward I (1272–1307), now held amongst the Campbell Charters in the British Museum. At that time the church was dedicated to St Radegund, who came from Thuringia (now part of Germany) she died in 587 AD. The date of the change of dedication is not known.

The tower arch is thought to be the oldest part of the present building. The north aisle dates from the 15th century and, apart from the part behind the organ, was unaffected by the 19th-century renovations. A mediaeval grave-cover forms part of the sill of the west window of the north aisle.

The north door, or devil's door, was blocked up at one time, then re-opened at a later date. The devil's door was kept open during baptisms to let out any evil spirits in the child.

Both the north and south nave arcades probably date from the late 14th century. There are two gravestones on the north side of the chancel, under the organ seat. One refers to the Jermyns, a wealthy family who owned property in Hackenthorpe, Eckington, and Drakehouse in Beighton.

Two brasses on the south wall of the nave, near to the squint (a window cut in the chancel wall to enable worshippers, or a second priest in a side aisle, to see the priest's actions in the chancel or sanctuary), proclaim the resting places of William Jessoppe, vicar of Beighton, who died in 1667 and M. Robert Jessoppe of Waterthorp Gent who died in 1753. Both brasses disappeared in the 18th century, however, they were found by the Reverend A.B. Maughan (vicar of Beighton from 1911–32) in a second-hand shop in Whitby and were restored to the church.

The Roman Catholic Cathedral of St Marie

Norfolk Row

St Marie's Roman Catholic Church was built in Norfolk Row, in the town centre, between 1846 and 1850 to a design by Weightman & Hadfield in Gothic Revival style and cruciform plan. It was built by John Pearson of Hanover Street and was financed by the Duke of Norfolk. A Lady Chapel was added in 1878-89 as designed by M.E. Hadfield & Sons.

In 1707 a building called the 'Lord's House' was constructed at the corner of Norfolk Row and Fargate, it was used as a residence for the agent of the Duke of Norfolk. Attached to the Lord's House was a chapel which was used for worship by the Duke on his visits to Sheffield and also by the Roman Catholic congregation of about 300. The Lord's House was demolished in 1814 but the chapel remained for another two years, when a new, larger, chapel was built.

St Marie's was built on the site of this chapel and the graveyard. The interior is rich in carvings and sculptures. The marble altar was executed by Boulton, and other sculptures by Thomas Earp. Wood carvings of figures in the rood, the chancel stalls, ten angels in the chancel roof, and the pulpit were by Arthur Hayball of Sheffield. Other work was done by the Sheffield artist Henry Taylor Bulmer. Gates, screens and railings by James and Charles Ellis of George Street, Sheffield. Frank Tory (see also St John's Ranmoor) sculpted the Pieta in 1887. The floor tiles in the chancel, the

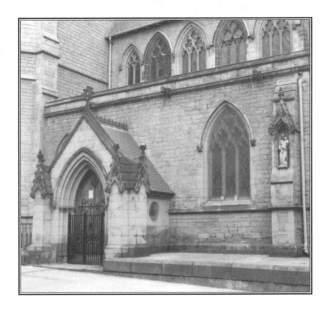

Blessed Sacrament chapel and the Norfolk chantry were designed and supplied by Minton & Company of Stoke-on-Trent. The organ, by Thomas Lewis of London, was installed in the chancel in 1875.

St Marie's is rich in stained glass. When opened in 1850, several windows had already been installed by Wailes of Newcastle, others have been added at various times.

Further details can be found in *The Lord's House* by Denis Evinson.

The church was made a cathedral in 1980.

Terminal Warehouse

Sheffield Canal Basin

The Terminal Warehouse is at the end of the Sheffield & South Yorkshire Navigation, at the Canal Basin now known as Victoria Quays. It was the first warehouse to be built on completion of the Sheffield and Tinsley canal in 1819.

Towards the end of the Napoleonic Wars, by act of Parliament passed in 1815, a navigable waterway was to be built to extend the canal system from Tinsley, at the end of the River Dun Navigation, right into the town centre at the end of Sheaf Street.

'Sheffield size' wooden sailing keels carried their various bulk cargoes to the canal basin or to the wharves of the factories alongside the canal. Many barges were horse-drawn into Sheffield, as the sails had to be lowered to get under the fixed bridges. There was stabling for 10 horses, below road level, adjacent to the end warehouse.

Many goods were imported and came to Sheffield via Hull Docks, the Humber and River Trent before entering the canal system at Keadby. The Terminal Warehouse received mainly cargoes of grain, sugar and tinned food, but items like dried milk, desiccated coconut and almonds were destined for Bassett's sweet factory. The keels went into the archway of the Terminal Warehouse and from here the goods were unloaded directly by crane and hoisted up through the warehouse to the required floor for storage. Spiral chutes at each end of the warehouse were used for transferring the produce to the road vehicles below for distribution in the city.

The last cargo into the Sheffield Canal Basin, in December 1970, was maize. For the following 20 years the basin was used only for mooring private boats, some of which were lived in as houseboats. There was a small boatyard for repairs and in the summer short boat rides down to the Tinsley Locks were offered.

The buildings lay empty and derelict. Several schemes to restore the basin were given consent by the City Council but they fell by the wayside during recessionary times. However, the dilapidated buildings have now being renovated for use as offices, restaurants, and small shop-units. New moorings and facilities, such as toilets and showers, have been provided for visiting narrowboats and cruisers, and the whole area has been rejuvenated and reclaimed mainly for the leisure industry.

On the same site can be seen several Grade II listed buildings, including the Straddle Warehouse and the Grain Warehouse which adjoins the Terminal Warehouse.

Turret House, The Manor

Manor Lane

The Turret House is situated near the main entrance to, and in the outer courtyard of, the ruins of the Manor, on high park land that belonged to the Earls of Shrewsbury, Lords of the Manor from 1406–1616. The most famous Earl was the sixth who, along with his wife Bess of Hardwick, kept custody of Mary, Queen of Scots, who was imprisoned by Queen Elizabeth in Sheffield for 14 years from 1570. The Scottish Queen was kept at the Manor for much of that time, alternating with the Castle, where she was first taken, and Buxton, where she went to take the medicinal waters.

The Turret House was built in 1574, probably to house the Queen with her retinue of many servants, their numbers were quickly reduced to thirty as an economy measure. It is the only part of the Manor which has a flat roof, so enabling the prisoner to take the air, watch the deer-hunting and admire the view of distant hills in and around Sheffield. The house consists of three storeys, each having two rooms. It also has many original features such as fireplaces, decorated plaster ceilings and strapwork, stained glass windows within stone mullions, and stone spiral stairs. Restoration was undertaken in 1873 and in the late twentieth century.

The Manor, two miles from Sheffield Castle, is thought to have been used as a hunting lodge, it was built by the fourth Earl of Shrewsbury and completed in the reign of Henry VIII.

During the 17th century the Manor fell into disrepair and in 1708 the Duke of Norfolk, who then owned it, demolished part and leased the site to tenant farmers, craftsmen and labourers. In 1907 the area was cleared of all but the surviving 16th-century and earlier buildings. Since 1960 the Sheffield Estates Surveyors Department have maintained the ruins and the Sheffield City Museums are making long term archaeological excavations and examinations of the foundations of the ruins. During drought conditions, when the grass area is parched, evidence of foundations under the ground are detectable.

According to Pawson and Brailsford's *Illustrated Guide to Sheffield*, 'Adjoining the ruins of the Manor there is a stone trough. This trough, it is said, was the coffin in which was buried the founder of Sheffield Castle, Thomas de Furnival. It was found at the demolition of the Castle, and on a stone forming the lid of it, it is said, was the inscription:

I Lord Furnival,
I build this Castle Hall,
And under this wall
Within this tomb was my burial.

The Manor is sometimes open to the public during summer months but often the gate is padlocked. Enquire from the Estate Surveyor's Department at the Town Hall. 0114 273 4697.

Arts Tower
and adjoining Library
Sheffield University, Western Bank

These two buildings are listed as good examples of the architecture of the period. English Heritage described the Arts Tower as 'The city's finest post-war building' and it is said to be the tallest university building in the country.

The University Library was built in 1959 and the Arts Tower in 1962–65, to designs by Gollins, Melvin, Ward & Partners. The two are connected at mezzanine level by a bridge.

The library is clad in Portland stone on a brick base and the glazing has a turquoise tint. It was built to cater for the 2,000 students who attended the University at that time, at a cost of £500,000 or £5 per square foot. It had then 200,000 books and 300 reading places. Now there are 18,000 students using 11 libraries at Sheffield University, 25,000 new books are bought each year. The most striking feature in the library is a silk embroidery, high up on the wall, depicting students at their graduation.

The Arts Tower is the tallest building in Sheffield, being 255ft above ground level in eighteen storeys, and a further 27ft in the basement below ground containing nine lecture theatres. It is fully glazed in both transparent and obscure glass panels with metal mullions and is flat roofed. It provides accommodation for the Faculties of Arts and Economic and Social Studies. Journeys between floors can be made on the continuously moving paternoster lifts, the fronts of which are open.

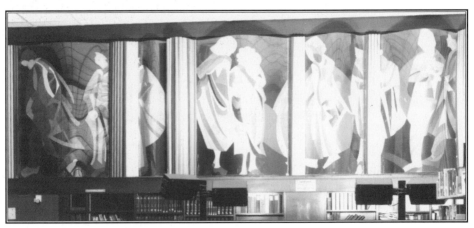

Silk frieze, University Library

The Arts Tower with the Library in the foreground

35 Well Meadow Street

attached Workshops, Ranges and Crucible Furnace

This consists of a house and attached workshops and a crucible furnace, circa 1840, with later-nineteenth century additions, and is to be found tucked away down a side street. The house has a central wooden-palistered doorcase with a cornice, and a door with an overlight.

The mid-nineteenth century workshop block has a vaulted cellar with six crucible holes and a coal-chute from the street. The picture shows the horizontal brick bands and vertical iron straps used to support the wall, to enable it to withstand the great heat from the furnace. This is the best surviving example of a building for small-scale integrated steel and cutlery making, from primary steel production, to polishing the final product in the adjacent workshop.

Details of this old doorway will be repaired and it will be retained in any future refurbishment scheme.

Wicker Arch
and adjoining Viaduct and Buildings

The Wicker Arches were opened on 12th December, 1848. They carried the Manchester, Sheffield and Lincolnshire Railway over 40 arches, 40ft high and 600 yds long, spanning the Don Valley. It is an outstanding example of early railway architecture.

The wide, elliptical central arch is 72ft long with small, round-arch footways at each side. It was constructed with huge ashlar blocks, the stone coming from a quarry at Wharncliffe Crags on the north side of Sheffield. The engineer of the project was John Fowler, and Weightman & Hadfield were the architects. There are four crests carved in stone representing: the M.S.&L. Railway Company; the Duke of Norfolk; the Earl of Yarborough; and the Sheffield Town Trustees. Under the south-east side pedestrian arch is a bronze plaque memorial (c.1920) to all the railway workers who lost their lives in the Great War, there are 1,304 names. The arches were restored in 1989–90 after the electrical gantry was removed. Now the line is only used for the occasional goods train.

At the north-west side is a viaduct of 12 arches, about 130m long, some contain workshops and some are bricked up. The south-east side led to the former Victoria Station (1851–1970) with a further 27 arches. Two arches span the River Don and others span Furnival Road, Effingham Street and Lane, and the Sheffield & Tinsley Canal.

Central arch and north-west footway

North-west side

K6 telephone kiosk, Leopold Street

Grade II Listed Buildings
in Sheffield

Abbey Lane–458, The Lodge
Abbey Lane–458, Boundary Wall and Gate Piers to Lodge
Abbey Lane–Ecclesall Woods, Charcoal Burner's Memorial
Abbeydale Road–387, Abbeydale Picture House
Abbeydale Road South–(Norton College, Abbeydale Centre) Abbeydale Hall
Abbeydale Road South–Post Delivery Office (100m NE of Church of St John)
Abbeydale Road South–Footbridge on Limb Brook, Ryecroft Glen (400m NW of Abbeydale Road South)
Abbeydale Road South–Woodland View, Licensed Victualler's Almshouse
Abbeydale Road South–Monument to Thomas Wiley (50m E of Woodland View)
Albert Road–20-42
Albert Terrace Road–Centenary House
Alderson Road–Sewer Gas Lamp (at junction with London Road)
Andover Street–Pye Bank School with Caretakers House and Boundary Wall
Andover Street–Seventh Day Adventist Church, adjoining School and Boundary Wall
Anns Road–Nursery, Junior and Infants Schools, Caretaker's House and Walls
Anns Road–St Andrew's Methodist Church and Sunday School with Steps and Wall
Archer Road–Park Lodge (former Police Station)
Argyle Road–Carfield Schools and adjoining Playground Shelter
Argyle Road–Caretaker's House and adjoining Walls at Carfield Schools
Argyle Road–Boundary Walls and Gates at Carfield Schools
Arundel Street–72, Butcher's Wheel
Arundel Street–92
Arundel Street–92a
Arundel Street–105, Venture Works
Arundel Street–113

Centenary House before restoration, former nurses home of the Royal Infirmary, Albert Terrace Road

Ashdell–Ashdell and adjoining Stable Block and Walls
Ashdell–Boundary Wall and Gate Piers at Ashdell
Ashdell–Sewer Gas Lamp (at junction of Ashdell and Westbourne Road)
Ashgate Road–6-20
Attercliffe Common–Attercliffe Chapel
Attercliffe Common–Tomb of Benjamin Huntsman (60m SE of Attercliffe Chapel)
Attercliffe Common–Carbrook School Workshops
Attercliffe Common–Boundary Wall at Carbrook School Workshops
Attercliffe Road–570 (former Trustee Savings Bank)
Attercliffe Road–580, Yorkshire Bank
Attercliffe Road–747 (former Attercliffe National School)
Attercliffe Road–749, Royal Bank of Scotland
Attercliffe Road–762 and 764
Bacon Lane–Canal Bridge, Sheffield & Tinsley Canal
Ball Street–Ball Street Bridge
Ball Street–Kelham Weir
Bank Street–18 and 20
Bank Street–22 and 24
Bank Street–26 and 28
Bank Street–30
Bank Street–36 and 38
Bank Street–40 and 42
Bank Street–44, Wharncliffe House
Bank Street–62, County Court Hall
Bannerdale Road–Church of St Oswald
Bardwell Road–Railway Bridge
Barkers Pool–First World War Memorial (25m S of the City Hall)
Barleywood Road–Pair of Chapels at Tinsley Park Cemetery
Barleywood Road–Lodge, Gateway and Boundary Wall at Tinsley Park Cemetery
Barleywood Road–War Memorial (250m E of chapels at Tinsley Park Cemetery)
Barmouth Road–Abbeydale House
Barnsley Road–Church of St Cuthbert
Beauchief Abbey Lane–Pair of Cottages (15m NW of Beauchief Abbey)
Beauchief Abbey Lane–Beauchief Abbey Farmhouse
Beauchief Abbey Lane–Farm Buildings at Beauchief Abbey Farmhouse
Beauchief Drive–Wall and Pair of Gate Piers (W of Beauchief Hall)
Beauchief Drive–Stable Block (100m W of Beauchief Hall)
Bellhouse Road–Church of St James & St Christopher
Bellhouse Road–Boundary Wall and Gates to Church of St James & St Christopher
Bents Road–55, Bents Green House and attached Boundary Wall
Bernard Road–Stables, Boundary Wall and Gateway (at Nunnery Goods Station)
Bernard Road–Horses' Sick Bay (at Nunnery Goods Station)
Bernard Street–Church of St John the Evangelist
Birch Road–5
Birley Spa Lane–Birley Spa Community Centre
Bishopscourt Road–Sewer Gas Lamp
Blake Grove Road–22
Blonk Street–41, Crucible Stack
Blonk Street–Blonk Bridge over River Don
Bochum Parkway–30, Jordanthorpe House
Bochum Parkway–Chantrey House
Bole Hill Road–Bole Hill Primary School and adjoining Boundary Wall and Shelter
Bole Hill Road–85, Caretaker's House (at Bole Hill Primary School)

Bole Hill Road–Boundary Walls, Railings and Outbuildings (at Bole Hill Primary School)
Bradway Road–46-52
Bradway Road–55, The Cottage
Bradway Road–Bradway Lodge
Bradway Road–Grange Farmhouse and adjoining Wall, Stables, Coach House and Barn
Bradway Road–Hall Farmhouse and adjoining Barns and Stables
Bramall Lane–331, Sheaf House Public House
Brightside Lane–Roadside Wall (facing main range of Vickers Building, River Don Works)
Brightside Lane–Vickers Building, River Don Works
Brincliffe Crescent–6, The Towers
Brincliffe Crescent–4, the Lodge to the Towers and adjoining Boundary Wall and Gate Piers
Brincliffe Edge Road–178, Woodside House
Brincliffe Edge Road–Sewer Gas Lamp (opposite junction with Union Road)
Broad Lane–James Montgomery Memorial Drinking Fountain
Brocco Bank–Church of St Augustine
Brook Road–Meersbrook Park and adjoining Service Buildings (City Council Recreation Department)
Brookhouse Hill–1, 2, and 3 Beech Dene
Brookhouse Hill–Christ Church
Brookhouse Hill–War Memorial and Railing (at junction with Canterbury Avenue)
Broomgrove Road–13
Broomhall Road–2
Broomhall Road–14, Park House
Broomhall Road–20
Broomhall Road–Church of St Silas
Broomhall Street–Sewer Gas Lamp (at junction with Westhill Lane)
Broomspring Lane–Grinding Hull (15m N of 120a)
Broomspring Lane–120a, Cutlery Forge and Assembly Shop
Broughton Road–31 and 33, Burrowlee House
Brown Hills Lane–Swallow Farmhouse
Brunswick Road–Boundary Mark (20m W of West Portal to Bridgehouses Railway Tunnel)
Brunswick Road–West Portal to Bridgehouses Railway Tunnel
Brunswick Street–50, Agnes Vere House
Burnaby Walk–189, Walkley Board School, Caretaker's House, Wall and Railing
Burngreave Road–189, Toll House and attached Railing and Wall
Abbeyfield Park–Abbeyfield House
Burngreave Road–Vestry Offices and attached Railings and Gates
Button Hill–Mylnhurst Convent School and adjoining Stable Range
Button Hill–Lodge and Gateway to Mylnhurst
Cadman Street–Attercliffe Sipelia Works
Cadman Street–Canal Bridge, Sheffield and Tinsley Canal
Cambridge Street–20 and 22, Leah's Yard
Cambridge Street–32
Cammel Road–Abbey Grange Nursing Home and adjoining former Stable Entrance
Canal Wharf–11-20
Canal Wharf–Grain Warehouse
Canal Wharf–The Arches and Linked Tunnel Entrance on Furnival Road
Canal Wharf–Straddle Warehouse
Carter Knowle Road–Carter Knowle Junior School
Carter Knowle Road–Boundary Wall and Railing (at Carter Knowle Junior School)
Carter Knowle Road–177, Caretaker's House (at Carter Knowle Junior School)
Carver Street–23
Carver Street–23, Scissors Forge in Courtyard
Carver Street–35, Dikkins and Le Metro

James Montgomery Memorial Drinking Fountain, Broad Lane

Carver Street–Wesleyan Methodist Church
Carver Street–Church of St Matthew
Castle Green–The Old Police Station
Cavendish Street–Springfield Junior and Infants Schools
Cavendish Street–Caretaker's House (to Springfield Junior and Infants Schools)
Cavendish Street–Boundary Walls and Railings (to Springfield Junior and Infants Schools)
Cemetery Road–294, Montague House
Cemetery Road–311, Sharrow Head House
Cemetery Road–Baptist Church and adjoining Sunday School
Cemetery Road–Gateway to General Cemetery with Screen and Flanking Walls
Cemetery Road–Old Chapel (Nonconformist) at General Cemetery
Cemetery Road–Monument to William Parker (40m SW of Old Chapel (Nonconformist) at
    General Cemetery)
Cemetery Road–Main Gateway and Lodges to General Cemetery
Cemetery Road–Monument to Mark Firth (60m E of New Chapel (Church of England) at the
    General Cemetery)
Cemetery Road–New Chapel (Church of England) at General Cemetery
Cemetery Road–Sewer Gas Lamp (at junction with Frog Walk)
Cemetery Road–Vestry Hall
Chesterfield Road–1 and 3, The Crown Inn
Church Street–5, The Royal Bank of Scotland
Church Street–17, The Midland Bank
Church Street–19 and 21, The Stone House Public House
Church Street–20, National Westminster Bank and Attached Offices
Church Street–Statue of James Montgomery (12m E of Cathedral)
Cinderhill Lane–Jordanthorpe Hall Farmhouse
City Road–Church of St Aidan and St Luke
City Road–Boundary Wall and Gate Piers (to Church of St Aidan and St Luke)
City Road–441 and 443, Gatehouse, Offices, Lodges and Screen Walls (at City Road Cemetery)
City Road–North West Lodge, Gateway and Boundary Wall (at City Road Cemetery)
City Road–Belgian War Memorial (at City Road Cemetery)
City Road–Roman Catholic Mortuary Chapel (at City Road Cemetery)
City Road–The Blitz Grave (200m E of Crematorium at City Road Cemetery)
City Road–War Memorial (80m NE of Crematorium at City Road Cemetery)
City Road–Crematorium and adjoining Chapels (at City Road Cemetery)
City Road–Manor Lodge School, adjoining Caretaker's House and Boundary Wall
Claremont Place–2, University of Sheffield Health Centre
Claremont Place–8
Claremont Place–10
Clarke Drive–Birkdale School
Clarkehouse Road–4-20 and 20a, with Steps, Walls and Railings
Clarkehouse Road–5
Clarkehouse Road–59, Broomgrove House
Clarkehouse Road–61-67
Clarkehouse Road–Gateway to the Botanical Gardens, with Lodges, Screen Wall and Railing
Clarkehouse Road–Crimean War Memorial (in the Botanical Gardens)
Clarkehouse Road–Lodge (near South Entrance to the Botanical Gardens)
Clarkehouse Road–Bear Pit (near south side of Botanical Gardens)
Clarkehouse Road–Warden's House (at Crewe Hall, University of Sheffield)
Clarkehouse Road–Stable Block (25m N of Wardens House at Crewe Hall)
Clarkson Street–1, Sheffield Centre Spiritualist Church
Clarkson Street–3, Beulah Kop
Club Mill Road–Sandbed Weir

Cobnar Road–Bolehill Farmhouse and attached Outbuilding
Cobnar Road–The Poplars
Coleridge Road–Crucible Steel Melting Shop (approx. 10m W of No. 286)
Collegiate Crescent–2 and 4
Collegiate Crescent–6 and 8
Collegiate Crescent–32
Collegiate Crescent–34
Collegiate Crescent–36
Collegiate Crescent–38
Collegiate Crescent–40
Collegiate Crescent–Sheffield Hallam University, Main Building
Collegiate Crescent–48, Lodge to Sheffield Hallam University Main Building
Collegiate Crescent–Wall and Gate Piers (to Sheffield Hallam University Main Building)
Commercial Street–5 and 7, Yorkshire Bank and Railings
Common Lane–Stable Block to Whiteley Wood Hall and attached Garden Wall and Gateway
Commonside–Moorfield Nursing Home
Corporation Street–Borough Bridge
Crookes–Wesley Hall
Crookes Road–91, Etruria House Hotel
Crookes Road–91a, Former Lodge, Gate Piers and Boundary Wall (to Etruria House Hotel)
Crookes Road–Steps, Terrace Wall and Gas Lamp (at No. 91 Etruria House Hotel)
Crookesmoor Road–Crookes Valley Methodist Church and School and Boundary Wall
Crookesmoor Road–Crookesmoor Middle School and Boundary Wall
Crookesmoor Road–143, Caretaker's House to Crookesmoor Middle School
Crookesmoor Road–Crookesmoor Vestry Hall and Caretaker's House (No. 80) and Boundary Wall
Crookesmoor Road–Unitarian Church and adjoining Boundary Wall and Bridge
Cross Burgess Street–Salvation Army Citadel
Darnall Road–Darnall School (now Community Association) Front Range and attached Boundary Wall
Darnall Road–Darnall School (now Community Association) Middle Range and attached Boundary Wall
Darnall Road–Darnall School (now playgroup) Rear Range
Darnall Road–Canal Aqueduct and adjoining Raised Footways, Sheffield and Tinsley Canal
Darnall Road–Lodge, Weighbridge Cabin and Boundary Walls (at Darnall Works)
Darnall Road–former Offices (at Sanderson Kayser's Darnall Works)
Darnall Road–Workshop (at Darnall Works approx. 40m SE of No. 20)
Darnall Road–Workshop (at Darnall Works approx. 30m SW of No. 20)
Darnall Road–287, The Ball Public House
David Lane–Hole in the Wall Farmhouse and adjoining Barns and Stables
David Lane–West Carr Cottages
Derbyshire Lane–Lodge, Gates and Boundary Wall (at N Entrance to Graves Park)
Devonshire Street–105-125
Devonshire Street–140-146, former Wharncliffe Fireclay Works and adjoining Showroom
Division Street–2-12
Dobbin Hill–304, Chestnut Cottage and adjoining Cottage to left
Doncaster Street–Cementation Furnace
Dore Road–99, Moorwinstow
Dore Road– Gateway and Flanking Walls (at 99,Moorwinstow)
Douse Croft Lane–Douse Croft Farmhouse
Douse Croft Lane–Granary, Barn and Cowshed (10m W of Douse Croft Farmhouse)
Drakehouse Lane–Sothall Green Farmhouse and attached Cart Shed
Drakehouse Lane–Barn and attached Farm Buildings (at Sothall Green Farmhouse)
Drakehouse Lane–Cart Shed (75m W of Sothall Green Farmhouse)
Earl Marshal Road–Earl Marshal Training Centre and attached Boundary Walls
Earl Marshal Road–Caretaker's House (to Earl Marshal Training Centre)

Earl Marshal Road–Electric Transformer (at corner of Barnsley Road)
East Bank Road–77 and 79, former Lodge and Screen Walls to Queen's Tower
East Coast Road–Sanderson's Weir (on River Don)
East Parade–2 and 3
East Parade–4-8
East Parade–9 and 10, Montgomery Chambers
East Parade–11
East Parade–12 and 13
East Parade–14, Office of the Industrial Tribunals
Ecclesall Road–Collegiate Hall
Ecclesall Road–1, Trustee Savings Bank
Ecclesall Road–1-18, George Woofindin Almshouses
Ecclesall Road–19 and 20, George Woofindin Almshouses
Ecclesall Road–Bridge and Lamp (12m SW of George Woofindin Almshouses)
Ecclesall Road–Boundary Wall and Gates (at George Woofindin Almshouses)
Ecclesall Road–Hunters Bar Toll Gate
Ecclesall Road–Pavilion and Lodge (at E entrance to Endcliffe Park)
Ecclesall Road–Statue of Queen Victoria (at SE end of Endcliffe Park)
Ecclesall Road–Jubilee Monument and Railing (in centre of Endcliffe Park)
Ecclesall Road–Jubilee Obelisk (at SW end of Endcliffe Park)
Ecclesall Road–Dam Walls at Sharrow Mills
Ecclesall Road–former Stables and Fan Room (to W of Sharrow Mills)
Ecclesall Road–Bridge and Retaining Wall (at rear of Sharrow Mills)
Ecclesall Road–New Mill building (at Sharrow Mills)
Ecclesall Road–former Stable Range and Cooper's Shop (to N of Sharrow Mills)
Ecclesall Road–Bridge and attached Gate Pier (to E of Sharrow Mills)
Ecclesall Road South–14
Ecclesall Road South–Banner Cross Hall
Ecclesall Road South–Terrace Wall (to S and E of Banner Cross Hall)
Ecclesall Road South–Ice House (150m SE of Banner Cross Hall)
Ecclesall Road South–Rubble Boundary Wall (to W and S of Banner Cross Hall)
Ecclesall Road South–Banner Cross Methodist Church and attached Rooms and Schoolroom
Ecclesall Road South–Boundary Wall and Gate Piers (to E and S of Banner Cross Methodist Church)
Ecclesall Road South–Church of All Saints
Ecclesall Road South–roadside War Memorial (80m S of Church of All Saints)
Ecclesall Road South–Central Block (at Hollis Hospital)
Ecclesall Road South–E Block (at Hollis Hospital)
Ecclesall Road South–W Block (at Hollis Hospital)
Ecclesall Road South–NW Block (at Hollis Hospital)
Ecclesall Road South–Parkhead Hall and adjoining former Stable Yard and Coach house
Ecclesall Road South–Whirlow Court
Edge Lane–Birley Old Hall
Edge Lane–The Falconry (at Birley Old Hall)
Edmund Road–Edmund Road Drill Hall
Edmund Road–Bollards and Kerb (outside entrance to former Drill Hall)
Effingham Road–Baltic Works
Effingham Road–canalside Warehouse of G.S. Dilley & Sons
Effingham Street–Crucible Steel Works (occupied by C.D.K. Precision Engineers)
Endcliffe Vale Road–61, former Lodge to Endcliffe Hall
Endcliffe Vale Road–61, Gate Piers (to former Lodge to Endcliffe Hall)
Exchange Street–Remains of Sheffield Castle beneath Castle Market (1)
Exchange Street–Remains of Sheffield Castle beneath Castle Market (2)
Exchange Street–Remains of Sheffield Castle beneath Castle Market (3)

Head Post Office, Fitzalan Square

Forbes Road–Owlerton War Memorial Hall

Forbes Road–Boundary Wall, Railing and Gates (at Owlerton War Memorial Hall)

Fox Hill Crescent–The Orchard and adjoining Stable

Fox Hill Road–Sewer Gas Lamp (at junction with Camborne Road)

Fulwood Road–Oakbrook (Notre Dame School Sixth Form Block)

Fulwood Road–375, Lodge (to Oakbrook)

Fulwood Road–446 and 448

Fulwood Road–450 and 452

Fulwood Road–454 and 456

Fulwood Road–458

Fulwood Road–460 and 462

Fulwood Road–464

Fulwood Road–Garden Alcove, Steps and adjoining Potting Sheds (50m SE of No. 381)

Fulwood Road–K6 Telephone Kiosk (at junction with Tom Lane)

Fulwood Road–Nether Green Middle School

Fulwood Road–Boundary Wall, Railing and Gates (to Nether Green Middle School)

Fulwood Road–The Guildhall

Garden Street–52, 54 and 56, and adjoining Workshops

Gell Street–34, Annexe to Jessop Hospital for Women

Gell Street–94

Gell Street–98

Gell Street–100 and 102

George Street–12 and 14

George Street–35

George Street–16

Gleadless Common–107, Commonside Farmhouse and adjoining Farm Buildings

Gleadless Road–Christ Church

Gleadless Road–Boundary Wall and Gates (to Christ Church)

Gleadless Road–Memorial to John Shortridge (15m SW of Christ Church)

Gleadless Road–former Wesleyan Methodist Church

Glossop Road–255-261

Glossop Road–267

Glossop Road–269 and 271

Glossop Road–273 and 275

Glossop Road–277 and 279

Glossop Road–281 and 283

Glossop Road–285

Glossop Road–287 and 289

Glossop Road–299, Area Health Authority Mental Handicap Services (Brunswick House)

Glossop Road–305

Glossop Road–319 and 321

Glossop Road–329-335

Glossop Road–338 and 340, Lloyds Bank

Glossop Road–342

Glossop Road–344 and 346

Glossop Road–348 and 350

Glossop Road–356

Glossop Road–361, 363, and365

Glossop Road–367-373

Glossop Road–375-385

Glossop Road–440

Glossop Road–463, West Mount and attached Wall

Glossop Road–457, former Caretaker's House (45m NE of King Edward VII School)

Glossop Road–Gate Piers (20m NW of No. 457)
Glossop Road–Memorial to Robert Ernest (20m SE of Royal Hallamshire Hospital)
Glossop Road–Somme Barracks
Glossop Road–University Drama Studio and attached Walls and Railings
Graham Road–229, Storth Oaks and adjoining Stable Range and Gateway
Graham Road–Riverdale House and adjoining Outbuildings and Walls
Graham Road–Lodge (to Riverdale House)
Graham Road–Gate Piers (2m to right of former Lodge to Riverdale House)
Granville Road–Entrance Lodge (to Norfolk Park)
Granville Road–Gateway and Screen Walls (at entrance to Norfolk Park)
Granville Road–Lamp Standard (at entrance to Norfolk Park)
Green Lane–Brooklyn Works
Green Lane–86 and 88, Wharncliffe Works
Greystones Hall Road–Greystones Hall Rest Home
Greystones Road–Electric Transformer (at junction with Highcliffe Road)
Grimesthorpe Road–344, Carr Wood House and attached Wall and Gate Piers
Grove Road–Church of the Holy Trinity
Halifax Road–Hannah Rawson School
Hangingwater Road–Bridge spanning Porter Brook and adjoining Steps and Wall
Hanover Square–2 and 3, and attached Boundary Wall and Railings
Hanover Square–4 and 5, and attached Boundary Wall
Hanover Square–6 and 7, and attached Boundary Wall
Hanover Square–8 and 9, and attached Boundary Wall
Hanover Square–10-16 (consec.) and attached Boundary Wall
Harrison Lane–Fulwood Hall and attached Outbuildings
Hatfield House Court–2
Hatfield House Croft–1-7
Hathersage Road–Burbage Bridge
Hathersage Road–Packhorse Bridge (approx. 850m N of Burbage Bridge)
Hathersage Road–Fox House Inn and adjoining Cottage, Service Buildings and Stables
Haugh Lane–25, and attached Outbuildings
Headland Road–Cemetery Chapel (at Crookes Cemetery)
Heeley Bank Road–Heeley Bank Community Centre and adjoining Infant School
Heeley Bank Road–Boundary Wall, Railing and Gates (at Heeley Bank Community Centre)
Herewards Road–Grange Farmhouse and adjoining Stables and Barn
Herries Road–Goddard Hall
Herries Road–Railway Viaduct
High Lane–Newlands Farmhouse and adjoining Cottages, Boundary Walls and Railing
High Lane–Coach House and Stable (10m W of Newlands Farmhouse)
High Lane–Garden Wall (25m S of Newlands Farmhouse)
High Storrs Road–High Storrs School
High Storrs Road–Walls, Railings and Gates (to High Storrs School)
High Street–2, Barclay's Bank
High Street–8-24
High Street–13-23, former Sheffield Telegraph and Star Building
High Street–1, former National Westminster Bank
Highfield Place–St Barnabas House
Highfield Place–Wesley House and Boundary Railings
Hollins Lane–Hollins Bridge
Hollinsend Road–Christ Church
Hollinsend Road–Boundary Wall and Gates (to Christ Church)
Hollinsend Road–War Memorial and enclosing Wall (100m W of Christ Church)
Holly Street–Bow Centre and attached Railing

Holly Street–Holly Building
Holme Lane–25 and 27
Holywell Road–Greentop Circus Training Centre
Howard Road–St Joseph's Chapel
Howard Road–St Vincent's Presbytery
Howard Road–former St Joseph's School
Howard Road–Church of St Mary
Howard Road–Loxley College Walkley Centre
Infirmary Road–83 and 85
Infirmary Road–87, The Ski Lodge
Infirmary Road–The Roundhouse
Jenkin Road–Brightside Nursery and Infant School, Main Block
Jenkin Road–Brightside Nursery and Infant School, Nursery School and School House
Jenkin Road–Brightside Nursery and Infant School Railing, Wall and Gates
Jenkin Road–Church of St Margaret
Jenkin Road–Sewer Gas Lamp (at junction with Tipton Street)
John Street–Stag Works
Kent Road–Sewer Gas Lamp (at junction with Nicholson Road)
18, Kenwood Park Road–18, Lantern Theatre
Lady's Bridge–Royal Victoria Buildings
Lady's Bridge–Royal Exchange Buildings and adjoining Castle House
Ladysmith Avenue–14, The Edge
Lancing Road–Sewer Gas Lamp (N of junction with Cherry Street)
Langsett Road–Officers' Mess and Regimental Institute (to former Hillsborough Barracks)
Langsett Road–North-West Barrack Block (to former Hillsborough Barracks)
Langsett Road–Hospital and Area Railing (to former Hillsborough Barracks)
Langsett Road–Boundary Wall and Corner Towers North-West section (to former Hillsborough Barracks)
Langsett Road–Central Stable Block (to former Hillsborough Barracks)
Langsett Road–Guardroom and adjoining Wall and Towers (to former Hillsborough Barracks)
Langsett Road–Magazine (to former Hillsborough Barracks)
Langsett Road–Riding School (to former Hillsborough Barracks)
Langsett Road–Store (50m SE of Riding School to former Hillsborough Barracks)
Langsett Road–Mobilization Store and Squash Court (to former Hillsborough Barracks)
Langsett Road–South-East Barrack Block (to former Hillsborough Barracks)
Langsett Road–Boundary Wall and Corner Towers South-East Section (to former Hillsborough Barracks)
Langsett Road–K6 telephone Kiosk (30m left of Walkley and Hillsborough District Baths)
Leavy Greave Road–Jessop Hospital for Women
Leavy Greave Road–Sewer Gas Lamp (opposite junction with Victoria Street)
Leopold Street–1, 3 and 5, Leopold Chambers
Leopold Street–7
Leopold Street–K6 telephone Kiosk (at junction with Orchard Street)
Leopold Street–Sheffield City Council Education Committee Offices
Leveson Street–Norfolk Bridge
Linden Avenue–18, 18a, 20 and 20a
Linden Avenue–Church of St Chad
London Road–Highfield Library and adjoining Librarian's House
London Road–Highfield Trinity Anglican and Methodist Church and Boundary Wall
London Road–Lowfield Junior and Infant Schools and attached Caretaker's House
London Road–Rear Range (to Lowfield Junior and Infant School)
London Road–Boundary Walls, Railings and Gates (to Lowfield Junior and Infant School)
London Road–75, The Albion Public House
Longley Lane–Longley Hall
Loxley Road–former Malin Bridge Corn Mill

Malinda Street–60
Maltravers Street–Sheaf Works
Manchester Road–115, Kersal Mount and adjoining Service Wing
Manchester Road–115, Gateway and Boundary Walls (to Kersal Mount)
Manchester Road–Rivelin Mill Bridge
Manor Lane–Manor House (Remains)
Manor Lane–Detached Ruin (50m East of Manor House)
Mansfield Road–Chapel (at Intake Cemetery)
Mansfield Road–Lodge and attached Walls and Wash House (at Intake Cemetery)
Mansfield Road–Boundary Wall and Gates (at Intake Cemetery)
Mappin Street–Mappin Building and attached Railings
Market Place–1 and 3
Matilda Street–135-169, Truro Works
Mayfield Road–Carr Houses
Meadowhead–Church of Our Lady of Beauchief & St Thomas of Canterbury and the Presbytery
Meersbrook Park Road–Vestry Hall, Boundary Wall and Railing
Meersbrook Park Road–Drinking Fountain (150m E of Meersbrook Park House, Meersbrook Park)
Melbourne Avenue–1, Sheffield Religious Education Centre
Melrose Road–Cemetery Chapels (at Burngreave Cemetery)
Melrose Road–Lodges, Railings and Gate Piers (at Burngreave Cemetery)
Melrose Road–War Memorial Cross (400m NE of Chapel at Burngreave Cemetery)
Melrose Road–Lodge (at NE entrance to Burngreave Cemetery)
Mickley Lane–Brook Hall and adjoining Garden Wall
Mickley Lane–Stable and Coach House (20m SE of Brook Hall)
Mickley Lane–Cherry Tree Lodge
Middlewood Road–Hillsborough Hall, Public Library and adjoining Boundary Wall
Middlewood Road–Coach House and Stable (20m NW of Hillsborough Hall)
Middlewood Road–152, West Lodge (at Hillsborough Park)
Milton Street–96, 98 and 100, (H. Brook and Son Ltd No. 96)
Milton Street–Beehive Works
Milton Street–Taylor's Eye Witness Works
Moor Oaks Road–Sewer Gas Lamp (at NW end)
Morland Road–Herdings Community Centre
Mulehouse Road–Sewer Gas Lamp (at Junction with Stannington View Road)
Neepsend Lane–Hillfoot Bridge
Neepsend Lane–368, The Owl Public House
Netherthorpe Street–Netherthorpe Junior School and adjoining Caretaker's House and Walls
Newman Road–Church of St Thomas
Newman Road–Boundary Walls and Gate Piers (to Church of St Thomas)
Norfolk Park Road–88, West Lodge (to Norfolk Park)
Norfolk Park Road–Gateway and Screen Wall (at West Lodge to Norfolk Park)
Norfolk Park Road–Beech Hill with attached Coach House and Stable Courtyard
Norfolk Road–Cholera Monument
Norfolk Road–Shrewsbury Hospital Almshouses, Chapel, Chaplain's House, Infirmary and Wall
Norfolk Road–Pair of Lodges and Gateways (at rear of Shrewsbury Hospital Almshouses)
Norfolk Row–8 and 10
Norfolk Row–12-20
Norfolk Row–22, Hallam Book Centre
Norfolk Row–24 and 26
Norfolk Street–97, 99 and 101, The Ruskin Gallery
Norfolk Street–103, Trustee Savings Bank
Norfolk Street–109, The Brown Bear, Public House
Norfolk Street–111, 113 and 115

Chapel at Shrewsbury Hospital Alms Houses, Norfolk Road

Norfolk Street–Cathedral House
Norfolk Street–Upper Chapel (Unitarian)
Norfolk Street–Victoria Hall, Methodist Church, Meeting Rooms and area Railing
North Church Street–15
North Church Street–17
North Church Street–19, and attached Railings
Northfield Road–Hale Court and attached Wall and Railings
Northumberland Road–1
Norton Hammer Lane–7 and 9
Norton Hammer Lane–10
Norton Hammer Lane–11, 12 and 13
Nursery Street–Aizlewood's Mill
Nursery Street–New Testament Church of God and attached Boundary Wall
Oakland Road–Sewer Gas Lamp (at junction with Portsea Road)
Oaks Lane–Barn (at west entrance to Concord Park)
Ouseburn Road–Kettlebridge Nursery First School
Ouseburn Road–Railing and Gates (at Kettlebridge Nursery First School)
Ouseburn Street–21, Caretaker's House and Gateways (at Kettlebridge Nursery First School)
Page Hall Road–18, 20 and 22
Park Crescent–1 and 2, Hyde Villas
Park Crescent–3 and 4, Hyde Place
Park Grange Road–Queen's Tower
Park Grange Road–Terrace Wall, Gateway and Stair (to west of Queen's Tower)
Park Grange Road–Service Wing and Cottage (at Queen's Tower)
Park Grange Road–Squash Club, former Stable Court (to east of Queen's Tower)

Cholera Monument, Norfolk Road

Lamp standard at entrance to Norfolk Park, Granville Road

Queen's Tower, Park Grange Road

Park Lane–4
Park Lane–Sewer Gas Lamp (25m SE of junction with Antrim Avenue)
Parkside Road–Hillsborough Nursery, First and Middle Schools and Walls, Railings and Outbuildings
Parkside Road–104, Hillsborough House and attached Boundary Walls, Railings and Outbuildings
Parkside Road–Caretaker's House (at Hillsborough Schools)
Parkside Road–Rear Range (at Hillsborough Schools)
Peel Terrace–1-6
Penistone Road–Church of St John the Baptist and attached Boundary Walls and Gates
Penistone Road–947, East Lodge (to Hillsborough Park)
Penistone Road–947, Gateway and Boundary Wall (at East Lodge to Hillsborough Park)
Penistone Road–Globe Works
Pinfold Street–Two K6 Telephone Kiosks (3m NE of Steel City House)
Pinstone Street–87 and 89, Prudential Assurance Building
Pisgah House Road–17
Pitsmoor Road–249 and 251
Pitsmoor Road–253
Pitsmoor Road–257, Christ Church Vicarage
Pitsmoor Road–259
Pitsmoor Road–Christ Church
Pomona Street–Bow Works
Pond Street–Howard Hotel and attached Shop and Workshops
Princess Street–Pluto Works

Psalter Lane–Psalter Lane Methodist Church and adjoining Steps and Walls
Psalter Lane–Boundary Walls and Gate Piers (at Psalter Lane Methodist Church)
Queen Street–68 and 70, Queen Street Chambers
Queen Street–72
Queen's Road–635, Trustee Savings Bank
Quiet Lane–Barn (20m NW of New Carr Houses)
Rails Road–Packhorse Bridge (70m E of Rails Road Bridge)
Randall Street–Portland Works
Regent Terrace–15
Richmond Road–Pair of Gate Piers (at entrance to Nos. 304 -330)
Ringinglow Road–Norfolk Arms Public House
Ringinglow Road–Ringinglow Roundhouse
Ringinglow Road–2, The Yews, Holly Cottage and adjoining Boundary Wall
Ringinglow Road–Upper Burbage Bridge East (that part in Sheffield CP)
Ringinglow Road–Upper Burbage Bridge West (that part in Sheffield CP)
Rivelin Valley Road–Coppice House Farmhouse
Rivelin Valley Road–former King Edward VII Orthopaedic Hospital
Rivelin Valley Road–Boiler House (5m N of former King Edward VII Orthopaedic Hospital)
Rivelin Valley Road–Octagonal Building (30m W of former King Edward VII Orthopaedic Hospital)
Rivelin Valley Road–Entrance Lodge (to former King Edward VII Orthopaedic Hospital)
Rivelin Valley Road–Roscoe Bridge
Rivelin Valley Road–St Michael's Cemetery Chapel

Ringinglow Roundhouse and the Norfolk Arms public house

Rivelin Valley Road–Monument and Railings to G.H. Foster (7m W of St Michael's Cemetery Chapel)
Rivelin Valley Road–Walsh Monument and Railing (at Rivelin Glen Cemetery)
Rockingham Lane–Samaritans' Office, former Methodist Sunday School
Rundle Road–1
Rundle Road–North Lodge (to Swallow Hotel) with Boundary Wall and Gate Pier
Rutland Park–2, Ornamental Chimney (No. 2 not included)
Rutland Park–8, Sheffield High School for Girls
Rutland Park–8, Boundary Wall and Gate
Rutland Park–10, Sheffield High School for Girls
Rutland Park–10, Boundary Wall and Gates
Rutland Park–10, Gymnasium and Music Room
Rutland Road–Rutland Road Bridge
St Aiden's Avenue–Arbourthorne Cottages north-east
St Aiden's Avenue–Arbourthorne Cottages south-west
St Andrews Road–Church of St Andrew
St Barnabas Road–11-17, Roundabout Hostel and attached Boundary Wall
St George's Terrace–Church of St George
St George's Terrace–Boundary Wall and Gate Piers (to Church of St George)
St James' Row–1, 3, and 5
St James' Row–7 and 7a, Old Cathedral Vicarage
St James' Row–9–14
St James' Row–15
St James' Row–16
St James' Street–4
St James' Street–8, Duke of Norfolk's Estate Office
St Lawrence Road–Church of St Lawrence
St Lawrence Road–Lych Gate and Boundary Walls (10m SE of Church Of St Lawrence)
St Mark's Crescent–4, St Mark's Vicarage
St Mark's Crescent–West Tower Porch (to Church of St. Mark, main body of church not included)
St Paul's Parade–Boundary Wall with Standard Measures
Sandygate Road–400, Holly Mount
Sandygate Road–The Towers and attached Garden Wall
Sandygate Road–The Lodge (to The Towers) and attached Gateway
Savile Street–48, Don Sawmills
Savile Street East–Entrance Gateway (to Thomas Firth and Sons Siemens Department)
Savile Street East–Atlas Works Offices
Savile Street East–President Works Office
Savile Street East–Firth's Norfolk Works, West Gun Shop
School Green Lane–30, Old School House
School Road–Sewer Gas Lamp (opposite junction with Globe Road)
Scotland Street–Chapel House and attached Hall
Senior Road–High Hazels House, Tinsley Park Golf Club, High Hazels Park
Sharrow Lane–1
Sharrow Lane–10, Charnwood Hotel and adjoining former Coach House
Sharrow Vale Road–Westbrook House (Sheffield Area Health Authority Offices)
Sharrow Vale Road–Westbrook Snuff Mill
Sheaf Street–Sheffield Station and attached Bridges and Platform Buildings
Sheffield Road, Tinsley–Sheffield Bus Museum and Sheaf Transport Garage
Shirecliffe Lane–Shirecliffe House (Parkwood College Department of Management)
Shiregreen Lane–Sewer Gas Lamp (at junction with Monckton Road)
Shore Lane–Tapton Court and adjoining Terrace Wall and Conservatory
Shore Lane–Tapton Hall and attached Terrace Wall
Shrewsbury Road–19, and attached Enclosure Wall
Silver Street Head–35, 37 and 39, Tree Tuns Public House

Snow Lane–Kutrite Works
Solly Street–216 and 218, with Workshop Ranges to the rear
South Parade–William Brothers of Sheffield
South Road–former Walkley Ebenezer Methodist Church
South Road–Walkley Public Library
South Road–Boundary Wall and Plaque (at Walkley Public Library)
Spital Hill–Spital Hill Works
Springvale Road–Crookes Congregational Church and attached Hall and Railings
Stafford Road–Boundary Wall, Gates and Railing (to Victoria Methodist Church)
Stafford Road–Victoria Methodist Church and adjoining Sunday School
Stannington Road–Meeting and Exhibition Room (on NE side of Mousehole Forge)
Stoke Street–Crucible Steel Works (at junction with Effingham Road)
Storth Lane–Electric Transformer (at junction with Belgrave Road)
Storth Lane–Overbridge (carrying Stumperlowe Crescent Road)
Stubbin Lane–Firth Park Methodist Church, adjoining Meeting Room and Boundary Wall
Stumperlowe Hall Road–Stumperlowe Cottage and adjoining Barn
Stumperlowe Hall Road–Stumperlowe Hall
Stumperlowe Hall Road–Stumperlowe House and Stumperlowe Grange
Stumperlowe Hall Road–The Barn
Stumperlowe Hall Road–The Grange Farmhouse
Suffolk Road–46, Columbia Place
Surrey Place–2, Sheffield Central Deaf Club
Surrey Street–41-49, Channing Hall with Shops below
Surrey Street–67 and 69
Surrey Street–Leader House and adjoining Boundary Wall
Surrey Street–The Surrey Public House and The Fringe Gymnasium
Sylvester Street–Sylvester Works
Sylvester Street–Workshop Range (to SE of Sylvester Works)
Taptonville Road–9 and 11, and attached Boundary Wall and Railings
Taptonville Road–13 and 15, and attached Boundary Wall and Railings
Taptonville Road–17 and 19, and attached Boundary Wall and Railings
Thirlwell Road–9, 11 and 11a, and adjoining former Bakery
Thomas Street–Taylor's Ceylon Works
Thompson Road–Gateway and Railings (to Botanical Gardens)
Tinsley Park Road–Youth Centre, former Board School
Tinsley Park Road–20, Caretaker's House and adjoining Boundary Wall (at former Board School)
Tinsley Park Road–Boundary Wall and Gates (at former Board School)
Tom Lane–109
Trippet Lane–23
Union Road–Kingswood Building, Nether Edge Hospital
Union Road–Left Lodge (at entrance to Nether Edge Hospital)
Union Road–(Right Lodge at entrance to Nether Edge Hospital)
Union Road–1, Union Hotel and adjoining Boundary Wall
Upper Albert Road–Sewer Gas Lamp (at junction with Rushdale Road)
Upper Hanover Street–80 and 82
Upper Hanover Street–St Andrew's United Reformed Church and attached Hall, Wall and Railing
Upperthorpe–Upperthorpe Public Library
Upperthorpe Road–113
Upperthorpe Road–115, St Stephen's Vicarage
Upperthorpe Road–117, Eversley House
Upwell Lane–Grimesthorpe Pump
Valley Road–19 and 21, former Joseph Tyzack and Co. Meersbrook Saw Works
Vicarage Road–former Adelphi Cinema

Victoria Station Road–Royal Victoria Hotel, Retaining Wall and Approach Ramp
Victoria Street–36 and 38
Victoria Street–40
Victoria Street–Church of the Nazarene and adjoining Boundary Wall and Railing
Vincent Road–Haqqani House Sufi Centre and adjoining Boundary Wall and Gates
Waingate–former Court House
Waingate–Lady's Bridge over the River Don
Well Meadow Street–54, and attached Workshop Ranges, including Crucible Furnace
West Bar–101-109, West Bar Fire Station Museum
West Bar–117 and 119
West Street–6-18, Steel City House
West Street–K6 Telephone Kiosk (outside Bow Centre Building)
West Street–98-104, Mortons
Westbourne Road–60, 'Ashgrove', Radio Sheffield
Westbourne Road–65, St Cecilia House
Western Bank–301
Western Bank–303
Western Bank–Gateway (at south-east corner of park in Weston Park)
Western Bank–Statue of Ebenezer Elliott (in Weston Park)
Western Bank–Yorkshire & Lancashire Regiment War Memorial, 1914-18 & 1939-45 (in Weston Park)
Western Bank–Yorkshire and Lancashire Regiment Boer War Memorial (in Weston Park)
Western Bank–Gateway (at south-west entrance in Weston Park)
Western Bank–Bandstand (in Weston Park)
Western Bank–Memorial to Godfrey Sykes (80m NW of Mappin Art Gallery, Weston Park)
Western Bank–Edgar Allen Building, Firth Hall, Rotunda and Quadrangle (at the University of Sheffield)
Westfield Northway–Waterthorpe Farmhouse
Westfield Terrace–13 and 15
Westfield Terrace–20
Wharf Street–12 and 13
Whirlow Lane–Whirlow Farmhouse
Whirlow Lane–Whirlow Hall Farm Cottage and attached Cowshed, Cruck Barn and Bull Pen
Whiteley Lane–Fulwood Old Chapel
Whiteley Lane–8, Chapel House
Whiteley Lane–Stocks (at Fulwood Old Chapel)
Whiteley Wood Road–Outbuilding, former Methodist Chapel (50m N of Meadow Lane Farm)
Whiteley Wood Road–4 and 6, Ivy Cottages
Whiteley Wood Road–8, Ivy Cottages
Whiteley Wood Road–Monument to Thomas Boulsover (on N side of Wire Mill Dam)
Wicker–46 and 48, Sadacca Social Centre
Wicker–85–93
Wicker–122 and 126 (National Westminster Bank No. 126)
Wilkinson Street–22
Wilkinson Street–24
Wilkinson Street–26
Wilkinson Street–27
Wilkinson Street–28 and 30
Wilkinson Street–32
Wilkinson Street–33 and 35
Wilkinson Street–34
Wilkinson Street–36
Wilkinson Street–38
Wilkinson Street–47
Wilkinson Street–66

Gateway to Weston Park (SE corner), Western Bank

Wilkinson Street–91-101
Wilson Place–10, Cruck Framed Barn
Wilson Road–Synagogue
Wilson Road–Succah (2m SW of Synagogue)
Wilson Road–Boundary Wall and Gate (to Synagogue)
Wincobank Avenue–Wincobank Undenominational Chapel and adjoining Schoolroom
Winter Street–Central Block (at St George's Hospital)
Winter Street–South-East Range (at St George's Hospital)
Winter Street–North-West Range (at St George's Hospital)
Winter Street–Lodge and adjoining Boundary Walls (at St George's Hospital)
Winter Street–Telephone Kiosk (75m to right of lodge at St George's Hospital)
Wood Cliffe–White House Farmhouse and adjoining Stable
Wood Lane–Wood Lane House Farm, Countryside Centre
Worksop Road–26, The Britannia Public House
York Street–1-9

Beighton

High Street–Manor Farmhouse

Dore

Church Lane–Christ Church
Church Lane–Croft House
High Street–5 and 6
Savage Lane–1 and 3
Savage Lane–Door Old School
Townhead Road–88 and 90, Cromwell Cottage
Townhead Road–94-104 (even)
Vicarage Lane–War Memorial (at junction with Savage Lane)
Vicarage Lane–Church Lane Farmhouse
Vicarage Lane–Memorial Lych Gate, Gateway and flanking Walls (25m E of Christ Church)
Vicarage Lane–Woodbine Cottages

Greenhill

Annesley Road–80
Greenfield Drive–Grange Farmhouse and adjoining Cottage
Greenhill Main Road–35, The Manor
Greenhill Main Road–35, Forecourt Walls, Gateway and attached Outbuildings (to The Manor)
Greenhill Main Road–43, Holly Farmhouse
Greenhill Main Road–45 and 47, Rose Cottage (45) and Croft Farmhouse (47) and adjoining
    Boundary Wall
Greenhill Main Road–59
Greenhill Main Road–61 and 63
Greenhill Main Road–Water Pump (adjacent to Nos. 66 and 68)
School Lane–3 and 5

Hackenthorpe

Beighton Road–Greenside and adjoining Garden Wall

Handsworth

Bramley Hall Road–Bramley Hall
Handsworth Road–Church of St Mary and attached Chest Tombs
Handsworth Road–Churchyard Walls, Piers and War Memorial (at Church of St Mary)
Handsworth Road–Handsworth Parish Centre and adjoining Stable Range, Pigeon Cote and Wall
Handsworth Road–Jeffcock Memorial Water Trough and Drinking Fountain
St Joseph's Road–Church of St Joseph and adjoining Presbytery
St Joseph's Road–Water Pump and Trough (12m S of Presbytery)
St Joseph's Road–St Joseph's Roman Catholic Primary School and Boundary Wall

Mosborough

Duke Street–2
High Street–Mosborough Hall Hotel
High Street–Service Building (at Mosborough Hall Hotel)
High Street–Entrance Gateway (approx. 70m W of Mosborough Hall Hotel)
Hollow Lane–156
Hollow Lane–158, Moss Cottage
Hollow Lane–Barn and Cowsheds (to N of yard at Mosborough Hall Farm)
Hollow Lane–Farm Buildings (to S and W of Farmyard at Mosborough Hall Farm)
Plumbley Lane–15 and 17, Plumbley Farmhouse
Sheffield Road–Wall and Gate Piers (250m W of Mosborough Hall)
South Street–31
South Street–33, Summerhouse and attached Garden Wall

Norton

Maugerhay–Chantrey Cottage and Chantrey House
Norton Avenue–Bagshawe Arms Public House
Norton Church Road–Preaching Cross (15m S of Church of St James)
Norton Church Road–Tomb of Sir Francis Chantrey (5m SW of Church of St James)
Norton Church Road–Memorial Obelisk (at junction of Norton Lane)
Norton Church Road–Norton Grange and adjoining Wash House, Stable and Boundary Wall
Norton Church Road–Stable Block (200m NE of Norton Hall)
Norton Church Road–Norton Hall Farm
Norton Church Road–Old Rectory
Norton Lane–Chantry Cottage
Norton Lane–Lodge (at Norton Nursery)
Norton Lane–Stable Range and Cottage (at Oakes Park)
Norton Lane–Pigeon Cote (10m N of Stable Range at Oakes Park)
Norton Lane–Garden Gate, Railing and Walls (30m E of Stable Range at Oakes Park)
Norton Lane–West Entrance Lodge, Screen Walls and Gateway (at Oakes Park)
School Lane–School House
School Lane–The Groom's Cottage
School Lane–The Post House

Totley

Butts Hill–Ash Cottage
Butts Hill–Cannon Hall
Hillfoot Road–5 and 7, Bryn Cottage (5) and Moor Cottage (7)
Hillfoot Road–Bridge (approx. 85m SW of Totley Grove)
Hillfoot Road–Bridge (approx. 200m NW of Totley Grove)
Penny Lane–Lower Bents Farm
Totley Hall Lane–Church of All Saints
Totley Hall Lane–Steps and flanking Walls (5m SW of Church of All Saints)
Totley Hall Lane–School House
Totley Hall Lane–Totley Hall
Totley Hall Lane–Totley Hall Farmhouse

Wadsley

Ben Lane–Dial House Club and attached Boundary Wall
Ben Lane–Loxley House (RN Training Ship Sheffield) and adjoining Service Wing
Far Lane–Wadsley Hall and adjoining Barns and Stables
Far Lane–Wadsley Hall Farmhouse
Rural Lane–239, and attached Boundary Wall
Rural Lane–Sewer Gas Lamp (15m S of No. 237)
Rural Lane–Wadsley Stocks (5m SE of the Wadsley Jack Public House)
Stour Lane–21, Rose and Crown Public House and attached Boundary Wall
The Drive–Wadsley House Club
Worrall Lane–Wadsley Almshouses
Worrall Lane–Wadsley Parish Church
Worrall Lane–Wadsley Vicarage
Worrall Road–Former Wadsley School Clubhouse

Woodhouse

Beighton Road–53
Beighton Road–53, Boundary Wall and Gateposts
Chapel Street–Trinity Methodist Church
Chapel Street–Gateway and Railing (to Trinity Methodist Church)
Cross Drive–Manor Farmhouse
Market Place–Cross Daggers Restaurant and attached Railing
Market Place–Village Cross
Market Place–Village Stocks
Stradbroke Road–Chapel (at Woodhouse Cemetery)
Stradbroke Road–483, Lodge (at Woodhouse Cemetery)
Stradbroke Road–Gateway and Railing (at Woodhouse Cemetery)

Bibliography

Bagshawe, Major & Mrs Thornber, *Oakes in Norton*.

Barraclough, K.C., *Sheffield Steel* (Moorland Publishing).

Bayliss, Derek, *Industrial History of South Yorkshire* (Association for Industrial Archaeology, 1995).

Historic Buildings in Sheffield (English Heritage & Sheffield City Council, 1995).

Hunter, J., *Hallamshire* (Pawson and Brailsford, Sheffield, 1819).

Lamb, Douglas, *A Pub on Every Corner* (The Hallamshire Press, Sheffield, 1996).

Lunn, Bishop David, *James Wilkinson-Vicar of Sheffield, 1753–1805*, (Lecture 1997).

Mee, Arthur, *The Kings of England*.

Ogden, Simon, *The Sheffield and Tinsley Canal* (The Hallamshire Press, Sheffield, 1997).

Pawson & Brailsford, *Illustrated Guide to Sheffield* (S.R. Publishers Limited, 1971).

Pevsner, Nikolaus, *Buildings of England* (Penguin Books, 1959).

Rayner, G.H., *The Cathedral Church of S. Peter & S. Paul* (British Publishing Company, Gloucester).

Tweedale, Geoffrey, *The Sheffield Knife Book: A History and Collectors' Guide* (The Hallamshire Press, Sheffield, 1996).

Vickers, J. Edward, *A Popular History of Sheffield* (E.P. Publishing 1978).

—Old Sheffield Town (Applebaum, Sheffield, 1978).

Walton, Mary, *Sheffield: Its History and Achievements* (Sheffield Telegraph and Star, 1948).